SCHOLASTIC

Early Reading
Instruction &
Intervention

A SOURCEBOOK FOR PreK-2

by Cindy Middendorf

New York · Toronto · London · Auckland · Sydney
Mexico City · New Delhi · Hong Kong · Buenos Aires

Teaching Resources

Dedication:

For Molly and Jackson.

Your sparkle, your joy, and your love of learning inspire me to see the amazing potential of all children. Thank you. May you always be blessed with teachers that care.

Love, Nana

Cover design: Jorge J. Namerow
Interior design: Melinda Belter
Cover photograph: © IStock
Development Editor: Joanna Davis-Swing
Editor: Sarah Glasscock
Copy Editor: David Klein

ISBN: 978-0-545-44276-3
Copyright © 2013 by Cindy Middendorf
All rights reserved.
Printed in the U.S.A.

1 2 3 4 5 6 7 8 9 10   40   20 19 18 17 16 15 14 13

Contents

Introduction 4

Chapter 1: Physical Readiness: The Prerequisite 8

Chapter 2: Interventions Within Whole-Group Instruction 37

Chapter 3: Tools for Best Practice and Interventions 48

Chapter 4: Phonological Awareness and Phonics:
　　　　　　　Best Practices and Interventions 68

Chapter 5: Sight Words 94

Chapter 6: Vocabulary, Fluency, and Comprehension 105

Reproducibles and Posters 136

References 142

Introduction

The demands upon the teacher in these days are of an extremely strenuous character. The multiplicity of subjects, the greater requirements as to qualification, the higher standards, and the greater results expected, all tend to make the teacher's work more important and more exacting.

—from *Practical Methods, Aids and Devices for Teachers* by Walter J. Beecher & Grace B. Faxon, Volume 1, 1916

L ook again at the date of the quote, which comes from a manual for teachers-in-training. 1916! Without exception, the burdens on a teacher have always been heavy. Honestly, the real differences between teaching in 1916 and teaching today are not as great as we may think. Yes, children in our 21st-century classrooms are typically closer in age to one another than they were in the classrooms of 1916; certainly, today we have access to more materials, technology, and equipment than did teachers in 1916; and few of us in the 21st century are responsible for starting the fire to warm the room before the children arrive! But today, as in 1916, the young minds in our charge span a range of backgrounds, readiness, and intellects. Just as teachers did in 1916, we deal with societal expectations, disciplinary issues, and concerns over our students who "just don't get it."

Goals, concerns, and challenges in our primary classrooms in the 21st century vary little from classrooms of nearly 100 years ago. No doubt the teacher in 1916 delighted in those students who were eager and able to master the printed word, just as we delight in the learners in our classrooms who learn effortlessly. But that teacher of 1916 most certainly agonized over the struggling students with poor reading skills, just as we do. Consider this quote from *Practical Methods, Aids and Devices for Teachers*:

> "Reading is the most important subject in any curriculum. In every grade there are methods of treatment for ineffectual reading. After the first question, 'Why does this boy or girl read so poorly?' comes the second question, 'How shall we teach so that this boy or girl will read more effectively?' Our aims should lie in a direct line with the child's development, and only along this line should we devise our mode of approach."

That 1916 insight, based on common sense and intuitive knowledge of how children learn, has now been validated by sophisticated research: "Our aims should lie in a direct line with the child's development." That statement is simply 1916 language for differentiated instruction. Devising a "mode of approach" for the child who reads so poorly? In today's world, we call it intervention.

Children and their experiences have changed dramatically over the last 100 years. Elevated societal expectations, varied family structures, and ever-changing cultural composition in schools have altered the face of education. But one thing remains constant: Good teaching is, was, and always will be about how children learn. And the fact remains that no two children follow the same learning journey. Never did; never will.

Today's primary teacher must be well equipped to discern the red flags that warn of a child's impending struggle and must be prepared to intervene at the first sign of distress. The old adage "Where there's smoke, there's fire" translates in the early grades to "Where there's a weak literacy skill, there's a risk of poor achievement." Research now confirms what teachers have known instinctively for a century: the earlier literacy interventions are in place, the more likely the skill deficits can be corrected. (Hausner, 2000; Manset, St. John, Simmons, Worthington, Chung, & Manoil, 2000; Velluntino, Scanlon, & Tanzman, 1998).

From preK through grade 2, we teach the mechanics of reading, always keeping in mind that the ultimate goal is to create readers of meaning, not simply "word callers." Our focus in the early grades is primarily on oral language, phonological awareness (especially that important subskill: phonemic awareness), phonics (including decoding and blending of words), and sight words. Once those basic, critical literacy skills are mastered and become automatic, early readers can use their cognitive energy to make sense of text. Weakness in those essential literacy skills, without intervention, snowballs into serious reading difficulties as children move into third grade and beyond where reading focuses on comprehension of content (Block & Israel, 2004).

The Response to Intervention (RTI) framework that is gaining traction in schools across the United States (as a result of a 2004 federal mandate) has earned credibility because of the overwhelming research confirming the need to identify and monitor struggling students as early as possible in their academic journey (Catts, 2006). Classroom teachers are now charged with providing initial, high-quality, research-based instruction for struggling learners within the general education classroom. Most RTI models refer to this as Tier 1 instruction. In most cases, Tier 1 teachers (the classroom general-education teacher) will modify and supplement instruction for struggling learners through differentiation, additional one-on-one or small-group support, and adaptations in the classroom environment (seating arrangement, study carrel, and so on). Those adaptations are typically called Tier 1 interventions. But remember, most are simply good teaching!

My goals in writing this book are the following:

(a) to put powerful, common-sense tools, activities, and strategies into your hands to ensure that your Tier 1 instruction and interventions are research-based, efficient, effective, and engaging, and

(b) to provide you with simple, useful literacy interventions that are helpful for all your learners, but especially crucial for those who are struggling, no matter what the reason.

What You Will Get From This Book

Chapter 1 peels the layers of learning back to the most rudimentary level: readiness. Every early childhood teacher knows that success in the early grades depends as much upon "RQ" (Readiness Quotient) as it does on IQ. Good luck teaching letters and sounds to a little guy who can't walk heel-to-toe, support his own body weight on his hands, or balance for five seconds on one foot! Chapter 1 helps you understand the crucial relationship between physical and cognitive readiness. You'll learn the reasons why we must pay attention to the important readiness factors of balance, sense of self in space, and crossing the midline. Also in Chapter 1, I share activities that are easy to embed into your established routines and transitions, which help develop both gross and fine motor strength.

Chapter 2 highlights whole-group teaching strategies that will benefit all learners, but are particularly crucial for at-risk students. Whole-group situations (discussions, listening to instructions, sharing ideas) are difficult for all young learners but especially taxing for struggling learners. You'll explore ways to keep all students engaged during whole-group instruction and learn how conscious, deliberate "teacher-talk" can be effective Tier 1 instruction for all children, while it serves as the necessary intervention some students need. You'll consider unconventional questioning techniques and whole-group discussion strategies that constitute solid, research-based instruction in the classroom.

Chapter 3 shows you tools for effective Tier 1 instruction. This chapter focuses on how we, the classroom teachers, can (and must!) intervene for a child who is exhibiting obvious signs of learning problems. You'll discover inexpensive, commonsense tools for supporting children who just aren't getting it, can't stay on task, or have attention issues serious enough to interfere with learning. This chapter helps you develop a repertoire of differentiated interventions that can help those children become more focused, more independent, and ultimately, more successful.

Chapter 4 outlines simple interventions for children who are deficient in basic literacy concepts and skills like phonemic awareness and phonics. You'll discover how incidental instruction during transition times can become second nature to you and your students. I've included tried-and-true strategies that sneak phonemic awareness and phonics into that dreaded monster, indoor recess. While the activities in this chapter are designed to provide practice and support skills for the struggling learners, you will learn (as I did!) that these differentiated center and independent activities offer effective reinforcement for all learners.

Chapter 5 is devoted to teaching, reinforcing, and supporting sight word vocabulary. This entire chapter gives you grounded, tried-and-true activities for supporting your differently abled learners (especially those with poor visual recall) in their mastery of sight words. This chapter offers suggestions to engage children of all readiness levels and learning modalities in hands-on, enriching practice for this critical literacy skill.

Chapter 6 helps you refine and revise your instruction for vocabulary, fluency, and comprehension. Even our nonreaders must develop skills that go beyond decoding and blending letters to making sense of text. This chapter is full of research-based instruction and intervention strategies appropriate for helping struggling and poor readers learn to find meaning in text and to connect text to their own experiences.

Throughout the book, you'll find examples of authentic work done by young learners, research, and reference resources to support your Tier 1 instruction, and typical classroom scenarios. Response to Intervention is rooted in differentiated instruction (DI). Differentiated instruction is rooted in brain research that confirms what good teachers have known for years: children learn in different ways. At its core, this book is about honoring that simple truth.

CHAPTER 1

Physical Readiness: The Prerequisite

Brain research confirms what teachers in 1916 knew instinctively: children need to develop physically if they are to succeed intellectually. Today it is easy to get caught up in the race for academic performance. But when we try to circumvent the natural progression of human development, we spend considerable time, money, and effort later trying to "fix" what we ignored. Whatever happened to readiness?

In the long ago days of Sally, Dick, and Jane, children began focused reading instruction in first grade. The children fortunate enough to attend kindergarten received a full year of readiness: gross and fine motor readiness, language readiness, social and emotional readiness. In today's schools, kindergarten's focus is on literacy, and even today's preKs give top billing to instruction in letters and sounds. There is no question that very young children can learn to read. Yet researchers are increasingly finding that unless certain crucial readiness elements are in place, reading instruction is less than effective. In the midst of the current academic pushdown, teachers must embed readiness in the early literacy experiences—not always an easy task!

If you are teaching kindergarten in this second decade of the 21st century, you are likely teaching the first-grade curriculum of the 1980s. Likewise, first-grade teachers today are teaching the second-grade curriculum of the 1980s, and so it goes. Emphasis on physical, social, emotional, and language growth in kindergarten has given way to emphasis on phonological awareness, phonics, fluency, vocabulary, and comprehension—all crucially important components of literacy, but ones that benefit learners who are *ready* for that instruction. Just as we can't install electrical wiring in a house before we lay its foundation and frame,

> It is a well established fact that Play is the child's most natural and inalienable right and one of the most potent factors in the development of his intellectual as well as his physical being. Through the medium of Play, we develop all his senses, train his powers of observation and concentration, stimulate his imagination, as well as give his little body the exercise and rest it must have.
>
> —from *Practical Methods, Aids and Devices for Teachers* by Walter J. Beecher & Grace B. Faxon, Volume 1, 1916

its walls, neither can we successfully teach a child to read before critical physical components (like balance, core strength, sense of self in space, ability to cross the midline, and so on) are in place.

High-stakes testing has resulted in an early childhood curriculum that is increasingly academic and skills driven. Increased emphasis on accountability and assessment has dramatically changed primary school curriculum, expectations, and appearance. Given a balance of rich experiences in the early years, physical readiness, and developmentally appropriate instruction in skills, children in the early grades *can* master literacy (Snow, Burns, & Griffin, 1998). But in a misguided effort to teach reading at a younger age, many curricula have turned kindergarten, first-, and second-grade classrooms into boot camp for the upper grades, complete with worksheets, paper-and-pencil drills, and long periods of seatwork. The result? Learners with no specific learning disability and no measurable neurological or intelligence deficit who struggle, who fall behind classmates, who soon question their own ability, and who, too often, become self-fulfilling prophecies of slow learners.

As early childhood teachers, we are dealing with the fallout from the pushdown curriculum. We say it over and over, "I know he (she) is bright, but something is just not clicking!" Take heart! Good news abounds! Research is now confirming that *children can learn to read well in the early grades* if:

❖ curriculum, materials, and instruction are developmentally appropriate, and

❖ physical and cognitive readiness are honored, acknowledged, and nurtured.

What Is Readiness?

Readiness is the unique point in development at which a learner can benefit from instruction. A teen may be ready for driver education only if (a) he or she is physically able to reach the gas and brake pedals and can see over the steering wheel, (b) has adequate visual acuity and perception, (c) has an understanding of road signs and driving language, and (d) has achieved the social and emotional maturity necessary to handle the responsibility. Similarly, a child entering school must have achieved specific physical, visual, emotional, and social milestones, as well as age-appropriate language development in order for our well-planned instruction to make a difference.

Cognitive readiness for literacy and numeracy includes letter and number recognition, phonological awareness, a sense of numbers, left-to-right sweep, and a host of other pre-reading and pre-math skills. But before a child is *ready* for skill instruction, he or she must be *ready* for learning. We know intuitively, and researchers have confirmed exhaustively, that learning is not solely a function of the brain. Physical development (and readiness) is intimately tied to cognitive development (and readiness), and many of our struggling learners need support in developing physical readiness.

In 2005, the National School Readiness Indicators Initiative published *Getting Ready*, a 17-state collaborative effort that researched and assessed the core factors of school readiness. First among the indicators of "Ready Children" stands physical well-being and motor development. That's no surprise to early childhood educators who know intuitively that our young students who have poor balance, who are unable to cross the midline, and who walk into things will struggle to learn letters and sounds. It follows logically that while we are offering these children differentiated strategies to master early literacy skills, we must also be continually bolstering, nurturing, and strengthening their physical development.

WHAT THE RESEARCH SAYS

Researchers agree: a powerful connection exists between physical maturity and cognitive readiness (Diamond, 2000; Hannaford, 2007). We now know that lack of attention to specific physical criteria can account for learning problems well into second grade and beyond, and that it's never too late to integrate activities for core strength, cross laterals, balance, and coordination. Some theorists speculate that the increasing incidence of learning problems in the early grades is directly connected to a cultural norm that no longer includes long periods of outdoor or active play for young children. The attraction of television and computers, concerns about safety, and complex family schedules all play a role in the lack of robust gross motor play that is crucial to building core strength, balance, coordination, and the sense of self in space—all now recognized as important factors in the readiness equation.

Early Reading Instruction & Intervention: A Sourcebook for PreK–2 © 2013 by Cindy Middendorf • Scholastic Teaching Resources

What Do Tier I Teachers Need to Know About Physical Readiness?

The physical factors most effectively supported and strengthened through intervention are also the same crucial factors that develop the neurological connections necessary for literacy:

- ❖ strength of core muscles
- ❖ ability to effortlessly cross the midline
- ❖ maturity of the vestibular system (sense of balance, visual integration)
- ❖ maturity of the proprioceptive system (sense of self in space, automatic timing of movements)

We early childhood teachers owe it to our young charges to understand *why* simply teaching and reteaching the skills of reading, writing, and spelling earlier will *not* make better readers, writers, and spellers by third grade. We need to educate parents, colleagues, and policy makers in our schools about the readiness factors that must come together before the youngest brains can make sense of letters and numbers. And we must know enough about how the mind and body function together as a unit to be able to defend our use of a developmentally appropriate literacy program.

We'll explore the role of each of these factors in learning. Later in the chapter, you'll find simple interventions that will support children who lack physical readiness. However, the activities are not strictly for struggling learners. All learners can benefit from them, and all learners should engage in the daily "brain-building" routines.

What is core strength? Why is it important to learning?

It's simple: core strength comes from the underlying muscles of the torso. Core muscles are those muscles of the trunk (chest and abdomen, the sides, and the mid- and lower back) that affect posture and stability. These are the muscles that are subtly, but vitally, important for everyday movements: walking, lifting, bending, even sitting and standing erectly.

Whether a child is standing, sitting in a chair, or cross-legged on the rug in front of you, his or her little body is continuously shifting and adjusting the core, sometimes noticeably and sometimes subtly. Energy is expended and muscles are exerted even as we sit still. Our body is continually redirecting muscles that have become too lax or too rigid. The stronger our core, the less energy it takes for our body to respond and react to those internal signals. Lack of core strength and development causes children to quickly become fatigued. They spend more energy reserves shifting, twisting, and readjusting, and therefore are less able to maintain cognitive focus.

Weakness in one's core makes engaging those muscles required for sitting still feel like hard work. Notice how many folks (children and adults) slouch in a chair after a few minutes of sitting, or hold their head up while sitting at a table, or walk with their head forward and shoulders rounded. Inadequate core strength leads to chronic poor posture. That in turn leads to an imbalance in muscles (some shortened, some lengthened), and that muscle imbalance impedes the strengthening of the core, which leads to poor posture. Talk about a vicious cycle!

Humans develop core strength from the neck down and from the core out. In a very predictable developmental continuum, core muscles strengthen, followed by large motor muscles (arms and legs), and finally fine motor muscles. Common sense tells us that before we can ask a child to hold and control a pencil (or scissors or a paintbrush), which requires fine motor precision, he or she must first have strength and control in the large (gross) muscles. We all know the frustration of teaching pencil grip to a child who can't skip! Gross motor exercises are not just for toddlers and preK. The readiness piece is this: *A child cannot have adequate fine motor function until he or she has adequate gross motor function; and gross motor function is dependent upon core strength.*

Impressive results are being seen in first-, second-, third- and fourth-graders who engage in consistent, frequent, purposeful exercises designed to stimulate specific neurological areas. For a fascinating probe into the brain-body connection and the impact on learning, read about the research-grounded program, Brain Gym (www.braingym.org).

What does crossing the midline have to do with reading?

Being able to cross the vertical midline of one's own body (perform a cross lateral) is an important developmental milestone. Most children who cannot *effortlessly* cross the midline of their own body with an arm or leg from the other side of the body will struggle with learning to read. That powerful fact is plain and simple, although the neurological reasons are complicated. Reading is a complex process that involves seamless communication between both hemispheres of the brain. Simply put, the left hemisphere decodes the words, turning letters into sounds, and sounds into words. The right hemisphere puts meaning and emotion to the words (Hannaford, 2007). It takes a lot of experiences with bilateral integration (using both hemispheres) to achieve the hemispheric teamwork necessary for reading with meaning.

In addition, efficient readers must visually cross the midline of the page as they track from left to right and from top to bottom. A child who is unable to cross extremities of his or her body over the midline will very likely struggle with tracking print.

Beyond reading, cross laterals are important in problem solving. Although most of us are predominantly right-brained thinkers or predominately left-brained thinkers, we know that our most effective, well-integrated, problem-solving moments come when both sides of the brain are communicating effectively with each other. When the brain "talks to itself," it is using all the resources of both hemispheres.

Each time we physically cross the midline of our bodies, we activate and strengthen a brain area called the corpus callosum. This incredible network keeps the two hemispheres talking to each other. Think of it as building a bridge from one village across a river to another. Each board that is laid makes the bridge stronger and travel between the two sides easier. When our young learners coordinate movements from opposite sides of the body (cross the midline), the corpus callosum receives input from both brain hemispheres and orchestrates integrated, balanced movements. A well functioning corpus callosum is crucial for reading, writing, and problem solving.

Crossing the midline also impacts other, broader aspects of learning. A child who is efficiently crossing the midline is most likely using both eyes and both ears, as well as both hands, in a coordinated, integrated way. Lacking that visual, auditory, and tactile integration (Dennison, 2006), a child will struggle with literacy. Many of the interventions later in this chapter include purposeful cross laterals.

What is the vestibular system and how does it impact readiness for learning?

Make no mistake: movement is crucial to learning. Hundreds of studies now confirm the important relationship between movement and thought process (Jensen, 2005; Hannaford, 2007). The vestibular system, housed in the inner ear, is a key player in movement as it gathers information and gives the brain feedback about our balance. It coordinates vision, movement, gravity receptors, and a host of other neurological activities.

Amazingly, the vestibular system is the first sensory system to develop after conception (Hannaford, 2007). It gives us constant feedback about our movements, our balance, and the constant pull of gravity on our body. Vestibular stimulation causes the rest of the brain to "wake up" for more incoming stimuli and encourages us to stay alert. Of notable importance is the relationship between the vestibular system and vision. The vestibular system makes it possible for our eyes to maintain a focus as we move our head and to coordinate eye and head movements. Without a healthy vestibular system, children struggle to learn.

Do your own research: Ask the children in your class to stand first on one foot for as long as possible, then on the other. You will probably find that most of the children who cannot maintain balance are also those who struggle with reading. Typical durations for age-appropriate balance are shown at right:

Ages 3½ to 4	8 seconds
Ages 4–6	10 seconds
Ages 6–8	30 seconds

To develop and maintain a healthy vestibular system, children need active play: running, spinning, climbing, balancing, and swinging. Because lifestyles today often limit outdoor play, many children come to school with underdeveloped vestibular systems, causing them to move, wiggle, twist, slouch, and generally seek vestibular stimulation. When the vestibular system is strong, the brain can stay alert without fidgeting. To strengthen the vestibular system, we must provide the balancing, twisting, gravity-defying stimulation that it seeks. You'll find activities later in this chapter that fill that need.

What does proprioception have to do with literacy?

You know the child. Jared (or Hayam or Sheila or Gracie) has something urgent to tell you (like there's a spider on the windowsill). As Jared runs to you, three bystanders along the way get knocked aside because he can't judge where his body is in relation to other people or objects. This same child often has difficulty sitting still, paying attention, and remembering abstract shapes (like letters and numbers). Learning to tie shoes is difficult, and pencil grasp may be limp and weak or fiercely tight.

Proprioception, closely linked to the vestibular system, is the body's ability to sense, adjust, and react to our body's alignment and position based on input from receptor points in our joints, muscles, tendons, and ligaments. It is our brain's unconscious sense of our body in space. Without proprioception, drivers would have to keep their eyes on their hands and feet to continually adjust them on the steering wheel and gas pedal. Proprioception allows one to walk up stairs without looking at each step, to type without looking at the keyboard, and to effortlessly get the spoon into the mouth when eating.

A child with a poorly developed sense of proprioception may exhibit some of the following behaviors:

- ❖ unusual need for cuddling, clinging, being physically supported
- ❖ avoidance of any "close your eyes" activities
- ❖ clumsiness, bumping into things, stumbling
- ❖ pronounced need for large personal space
- ❖ constant stretching

Please note that the "red flags" listed above can also be indicative of other physical and/or neurological issues such as sensory integration problems. Our bodies are ecosystems in which so many functions are interconnected that it's often difficult to discern whether underdeveloped proprioception is the result of sensory integration issues, or sensory integration issues result, in part, from poor proprioception. Either way, children with or without sensory issues will benefit from a well-developed, integrated sense of proprioception.

A child with weak proprioception uses so much neural energy, subconsciously seeking pressure on joints and muscles to determine body location, that little is left for the actual task of learning. Imagine trying to learn a new language while balancing on a tree limb or paying attention to a speaker while standing on one leg. Without the smooth eye movements associated with well-developed proprioception, tracking print, recalling visual images (like letters and numbers), and writing become difficult tasks.

All children will benefit from activities that engage and stimulate this important sense. But for children whose proprioceptive systems have not developed in an age-appropriate way, the activities become crucial interventions.

Intervention and Support Activities for Core Strength, Crossing the Midline, Developing the Vestibular System, and Activating Proprioception

The following activities can become a daily part of children's morning check-in routine, brain-break energizers, or transition activities during the day. All of the activities are quick, simple, and fun. While your ultimate goal is to provide intervention for children with weak core strength, proprioception, or balance skills, be assured that these activities are valuable for all your learners. Before you begin, make sure children understand why you are encouraging these workouts: "The more fit your body is, the more fit your brain is!"

The Push-Up Place

Materials: poster board and scissors or paint and paintbrush

Designate a spot on a wall or closet door where you can post or paint two handprints. Put two footprints on the floor a foot away from the wall. Direct children to stand on the footprints, place their hands on the handprints, and do push-ups. (Although I always asked children to do one push-up for each year of their age, they would always do more. Eventually, I had to set a limit so that everyone had access to the Push-Up Place.)

As children become stronger, encourage them to step off the footprints and move their feet farther back.

Early Reading Instruction & Intervention: A Sourcebook for PreK–2 © 2013 by Cindy Middendorf • Scholastic Teaching Resources

Extensions and Options: Instead of saying, "Push in your chairs and line up at the door," ask students to transition away from table or seat work by using their chairs as a quick, energizing way to exercise core muscles: "Stand behind your chair with your hands on the back of the chair. Count by fives to 50 (or 'recite the ABCs' or 'say and spell five spelling words') as you do push-ups off the chair. Too easy? Move your feet farther back."

Rationale: The ability to support one's own body weight is an important factor in physical development. All movement originates at the core, and a stronger core makes it easier to balance, to sit for extended periods and to maintain better posture. While you may have only two or three students who demonstrate weak core strength, core strength exercises are good for all your students (and for you, too!) So, while these exercises may be crucial and targeted interventions for specific students, consider them beneficial to all.

Push-Up Place *By regularly changing the skill focus on the Push-Up wall, children can count, recite nursery rhymes, read sight words, or practice spelling while building core strength.*

The Circle Circuit

Materials: poster board, marker, dry-erase marker, old sock

On a large piece of chart paper, draw a large circle. Inside the circle, draw a smaller circle, and smaller circle within that circle until you have three to five concentric circles. Put a large dot on the "two-o'clock spot" on each circle to indicate the starting point for tracing, and an arrow indicating that the tracing should be counter-clockwise.

Laminate the Circle Circuit and mount it on a wall or closet door at child-level. Provide a dry-erase marker in a sock. (The sock can be used as the eraser.) Direct children to trace and then erase all the traced circles without moving their feet. Remind them to follow their hand movement with their eyes. Insist that the erasures follow the same counterclockwise, big arm movements.

Extensions and Options: In addition to circles, create one large laminated X. Again, have children stand in one spot and trace from upper left to lower right and then from upper right to lower left. Or, instead of having children trace with a dry-erase marker, they could simply trace with their index finger (to eliminate the need to erase).

Rationale: This simple exercise develops the sense of self in space (proprioception) and gives children practice in crossing the midline. Before a child can cross the midline of the paper when writing, or cross the midline of a page with his or her eyes when reading, he or she must be able to cross the midline using large muscles.

Tracing the circles (or an X) requires large movements that anchor the core, activate proprioception, and integrate spatial movements. Working with hands and arms up, against gravity, builds shoulder and arm strength. Children whose physical development is weak will reap the most benefit from Circle Circuits, but the exercise is certainly worthwhile for all learners.

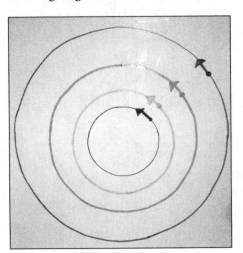

Circle Circuit *Insist that children keep their feet firmly planted while tracing the circles on this laminated board, and that they follow the tracing with their eyes. They'll cross the midline, develop visual tracking, and build large muscle strength.*

Beanbags

Materials: a beanbag for each student

Beanbags to the rescue for indoor recess or as a productive class energizer on a gloomy afternoon! Beanbag activities can be an intervention activity for physically immature children while allowing everyone to work out the wiggles. Ask children to stand in one spot as you gently toss the beanbag directly above their head (about an arm's length up) and to catch it with both hands. (Yes, you have to teach "gently." Yes, you have to teach "arm's length." And, yes, you have to remind Dominick, Justine, Sam, or whoever your Limit-Pusher-of-the-Year may be, that once he or she abuses the privilege of tossing a beanbag, the privilege of tossing a beanbag is lost!) After practice, encourage children to toss the bean bag up and catch it with only one hand. Ask them to toss it laterally back and forth between their hands. Very well-integrated children will be able to accomplish the lateral toss with their eyes closed. Finally, demonstrate placing the beanbag on your head and walking forward, backward, and sideways.

Extensions and Options: Mark a straight line on the floor with tape and ask children to "walk the plank" while balancing their beanbags on their heads. Then tell them to hold their arms out to the sides, palms facing up, with a beanbag in each palm. Challenge them to walk in a straight line.

Rationale: One must walk erectly to hold the beanbag on the head or in an outstretched palm. Walking erectly makes core muscles work!

Also, the vestibular system (sense of balance located in the inner ear) and the sense of proprioception are intricately connected to each other, and both are affected by—and impact—vision. Early childhood teachers know that the child who exhibits jerky, poorly coordinated movements, who walks into things and who has poor balance often is the child who struggles in learning. The earlier and more deliberately we intervene with exercises that support the vestibular and proprioceptive systems, the more likely that that child can catch up. The rest of the children in your class will benefit, too, since they will be reinforcing and strengthening critical readiness systems.

Rainbow Painting

Materials: crayons

Have children sit in their chairs with a crayon box, basket, or tub on the floor between their feet. As you name the colors of the rainbow, they will reach down, grab the appropriate color, and hold it as they would hold a paintbrush. Tell children to sit up straight and reach across their body to "paint" an imaginary arch beginning on one side, up over their head, and down to the other side. They should use only their arm, not their body! Encourage them to look at their hand the entire time. Repeat until they have "painted" with each color of the rainbow.

Extensions and Options: Ask children to alternate hands as they change colors. Encourage them to spell the color word (or a spelling word) as they create the arch. Instead of using crayon baskets, allow them to pretend that they have a bucket of paint that they must dip the brush (their hand) into before painting.

Rationale: The bending and stretching activates the proprioceptive system as it senses a limit to how far one can bend down before meeting resistance (the floor), but senses no limit in stretching upward. Holding the body still while painting the arch overhead is an integrated cross-lateral move. Tracking the hand with the eyes forces vision, balance, and sense of self in space to work together.

Ribbons, Scarves, and Streamers

Materials: ribbons, scarves, and streamers (for other options, see the sidebar), basket

Give each child a scarf, a length of ribbon, or a streamer. To begin, show them simple upper body moves: forward and backward arm circles, figure eights, or overhead circles.

As children smoothly and rhythmically move, they can be spelling words, saying the alphabet, reciting nursery rhymes, or keeping the beat to music. Emphasize moving only the upper body while keeping feet planted firmly, hip-width apart.

Extensions and Options: If you're fortunate enough to have another class set of ribbons, streamers, or scarves, give children one for each hand. Demonstrate how to cross your arms over each other to the beat of the music. Or, after using scarves, ribbons, or streamers in the classroom, make a basket of them available on the playground during recess. Children love to run with them!

MAKE YOUR OWN RIBBONS, SCARVES, AND STREAMERS

Dance scarves are available from many teacher supply sites and catalogs, but they are often too long for young children to smoothly manipulate. The same sites and catalogs usually offer smaller, less expensive versions most often called juggling scarves.

You can inexpensively make a class set of colorful streamers by simply tying five or six 12-inch lengths of ribbon or fabric strips (one-inch widths) to a ponytail holder or a scrunchie. Tie each tightly, near the end. If the ends ravel, cover them with a small piece of duct tape. (To prevent any fraying, carefully singe each end of the ribbon before tying it on.) Boys love camouflage fabric cut into strips. Children can hold the scrunchie or put it on their wrists to perform the activities. Making ribbon streamers is a great activity for parent volunteers or your parent support organization!

Early Reading Instruction & Intervention: A Sourcebook for PreK–2 © 2013 by Cindy Middendorf • Scholastic Teaching Resources

Rationale: There is a lot of proprioception and vestibular stimulation going on here! By keeping the feet in one place, a child engages only the core and upper large muscle groups. The wide range of movement provides great exercise for arm muscles. In addition, the movement stimulates the natural connection between eye movement and proprioception.

Leaning Towers

Two children stand facing each other, elbows bent, palms touching their partner's palms. Each child takes a small step backward, keeping their palms flat against their partner's palms. They continue to take tiny steps backward until they are supporting each other with their palms. Then partners begin to slowly step forward until each is standing upright again.

Extensions and Options: Reluctant children can be encouraged to stand still while their partner takes small steps back. Older children can stand side-by-side, shoulder-to-shoulder, and move their feet slowly to the side until their shoulders support each other's body weight. Or ask them to stand back-to-back and slowly walk out, causing their body weight to be supported by the partner's upper back.

Rationale: Core muscles are exercised, and both vestibular and proprioceptive systems are activated as the center of gravity shifts. In addition, this exercise requires children to trust a partner!

Eye Ballet

Materials: finger puppets or ribbons

Ask children to stand, while extending an index finger in front of them, pointing up. (Encourage them to extend the dominant hand.) Ask them to "air-write" a shape, letter, or number while standing in one spot and following the index finger with their eyes. Model using large arm movements to air-write while moving nothing but your eyes. Discourage head movement!

Extensions and Options: For younger children, or children who still exhibit jerky eye movement when tracking, provide a finger puppet to make the index finger more visually obvious. Or tie a colorful ribbon to their index finger. Young children

THE EYES HOLD THE KEY

When we are engaged in active learning, our eyes are in motion as we visually absorb external stimuli from our environment. Too often, children who struggle in the early grades have difficulty following their finger (or yours) as it tracks in the air across their entire field of vision. Their eyes may jump as they visually track in the air; they may complain that it hurts to move their eyes without moving their head; they may lose focus and have to begin again, or they may move their entire head instead of just their eyes. Before a child can be comfortable in visually tracking print from left to right, he or she must experience the world visually while engaged in large muscle activity that requires visual shifts from far to near and the coordination of vision with proprioception.

The 21st century lifestyle includes less robust, full-body, play-filled engagement for our young children. Safety concerns, video entertainment, long periods in car seats, lack of outdoor play areas, and a host of other factors have impacted visual development.

Very young children have strong three-dimensional and peripheral vision. Vision and movement work together to strengthen eye muscles when a child is outside running, climbing, and swinging. Without adequate muscular development in the eyes, children struggle when transitioning from that three-dimensional, strong peripheral vision to the two-dimensional, bifoveal vision needed to process static text on a page, the very visual process that is required for school success. Instead of a natural, smooth transition, the eyes often experience a sudden, stressing shift. The result is jerky eye movements and vision that doesn't smoothly track across a page, making reading difficult. The bottom line: movement, crucial for so many strong brain connections, is also imperative for functional vision.

love a ring on the finger. As children become more competent, ask them to draw a "lazy eight," that is, the numeral eight turned sideways. A child who can visually track a lazy eight with effortless and smooth movements usually has no trouble tracking print on a page.

Rationale: Fluent, convergent eye teaming is a prerequisite for competency in reading. The more smoothly the eyes work together, the more the eye muscles strengthen, and the more connections to the brain are available through the proprioceptive and vestibular systems (Hannaford, 2007). In addition, when the head is kept still and the finger moves through a wide visual field, the eyes must cross the midline of the body as they track. This activates and strengthens the corpus callosum, which lets the left hemisphere and the right hemisphere communicate, allowing words (decoded by the left hemisphere) to have meaning (pictured in the right hemisphere).

Chair Workout

How many times a day do you say, "Stand up and push in your chairs"? Take an additional 10 seconds to automatically include some quick core strengthening, as well as vestibular and proprioceptive stimuli. Say instead, "Chair workouts!" Children will automatically stand and push in their chairs, since the chair must be stable against the desk or table to accomplish a chair workout. Have them stand behind the chair and do push-ups against it, with their feet as far from the chair as possible, based on furniture arrangement in the room and the child's own core strength. Obviously, the longer the distance from the chair to their feet, the stronger their arms and core muscles must be to do a push-up.

Extensions and Options: To work on balance and proprioception, ask children to stand behind the chair and lift one leg off the floor by bending their knee. They may use the chair for stability if necessary. Then they do the same with the opposite leg. As children get better at this, ask them to close their eyes while they balance on one foot. Challenge them to pull the lifted knee up as high as possible while standing erect.

Rationale: This fast exercise activates several brain areas that are necessary for optimum learning and that become less active during seatwork. Think of it as a vitamin supplement for learning. Since we know that core strength and the vestibular and proprioceptive systems are intricately involved in learning, why wouldn't we take every opportunity to fortify them?

Purposeful Hall Walking

Incorporate movement with a purpose as you lead your students to a different area of the building. For short distances, use Heel-to-Toe walking. You'll find most students will extend their arms to maintain balance. Or ask children to do the Penguin Walk, keeping their knees and elbows stiff, feet turned out slightly. (Try it and feel yourself tighten your core muscles!) Model how to do Side Lifts while walking. (Pretend you have an exercise weight in each hand. Hold your fists—with imaginary weights—so they touch the outside of your shoulders. Now extend them sideways with slow deliberate movements, moving your arms in sync with the steps. Challenge students to do a graceful Juggle Walk, deftly juggling imaginary balls and keeping their eyes on the balls as they walk.

Extensions and Options: When necessary, modify the movements for less-coordinated students. (Heel-to-Toe walking might start out as Feet-in-a-Straight-Line; Penguin Walk might require only arms to be held stiff; Side Lifts might be Alternate Side Lifts.)

As their competence and coordination increase, ask children to walk while lightly slapping the opposite thigh with each step. (The right hand slaps the left thigh when the left foot is extended; the left hand slaps the right thigh when the right foot is extended.) Challenge more adept children to lift their knees high, touching opposite elbows to opposite knees.

These engaging walks can also be used within the classroom as you ask children to move from centers to seats or from the story rug to the closet or cubbies. Without a doubt, some of the intentional movements suggested are easier than others, and you alone know where your class should begin. You will soon discover your own Purposeful Walking activities, and children will be eager to suggest their favorites.

Rationale: Welcome interlude! It's time to walk children to music, gym, lunch, or another activity in your schedule that gives you a few free minutes to organize centers, rediscover your desk, dash off a parent note, or prepare materials for a lesson. But first you must deliver your class to the assigned spot without disrupting other classes. The purposeful hall walking activities involve core strength, crossing the midline, maintaining balance, or a combination of these important physical integrations. Time spent transitioning from room to room can be valuable brain/body-building time. Think of it as another vitamin supplement for healthy brains! The bonus is, that while children are focusing on their own body movements, they're not at-risk for mischief!

Brain Breaks That Energize

Getting and keeping the attention of 20-some young learners requires skill, talent, and a healthy dose of patience. Young brains are not designed for long periods of focused attention, a fact that is certainly not news to any early childhood

Early Reading Instruction & Intervention: A Sourcebook for PreK–2 © 2013 by Cindy Middendorf • Scholastic Teaching Resources

teacher. Researchers tell us that *all* learners, young and old, function best when the brain is periodically energized through movement at 10- to 20-minute intervals (Jensen, 2007). Besides increasing blood flow to the brain, movement (especially movement that accelerates the heart rate) releases endorphins, a natural "feel-good" neurotransmitter.

The following energizers may be the intervention that is needed for some of those besieged young brains to refresh themselves, refocus their thoughts, and prepare for what's coming. All your children will enjoy regular brain breaks; your struggling learners must have them!

Energizer #1: Flamingo Stand: Have children do the following: Stand. Lift one foot, balancing on the other. Hold it for 5–10 seconds (perhaps while spelling a given word or reading several sight words or reciting number facts). Change feet and repeat. Remind children to breathe deeply!

Energizer #2: Pencil Stance: While children are in a standing position, tell them to cross their ankles and keep their feet flat on the floor. Then have students raise their arms straight overhead and hook their thumbs. Encourage them to hold this position for several seconds. Try it again, having children cross their ankles in the opposite way (the front ankle becomes the back ankle). Remind them to breathe while holding the stance.

Energizer #3: Static Hand Push: Have students put their hands in "prayer position" with their forearms at a 90-degree angle to their hands and thumbs, at about chin level. Ask them to push their hands as hard as they can against each other. Challenge children to hold the position for about 10 seconds, relax, and then repeat.

Energizer # 4: Finger Match: Ask children to stand, raise their hands overhead and touch all five fingers of one hand to the corresponding fingers on the other hand. As competence increases, ask them to touch index finger to index finger, pinky to pinky, thumb to thumb, and so on.

Energizer #5: Car and Driver: Pair students. One child is the car; one is the driver. Driver places hands on the shoulders of Car; Car closes his or her eyes. Driver "steers" Car around the room, slowly and deliberately, to navigate around desks. Then have pairs switch roles.

Energizer #6: Juggling: For this activity, hand out a beanbag or small beanie baby, koosh ball, or stuffed sock to each child. Ask children to toss it over their heads (only about a foot) with one hand, and to catch it with the other. Repeat for one or two minutes. Tell children to alternate the "tossing" and "catching" hands. Extend this by asking them to toss the beanbag back and forth between their hands while slowly moving their hands farther and farther apart.

Materials: beanbag, small beanie baby, koosh ball, or stuffed sock for each child

Energizer #7: Backslap: Model this activity for children: From a standing position, tap your left heel with your right palm behind you, keeping beat to music. Alternate.

Energizer #8: Walking Backward: A minute or two of backward walking wakes up the body and the brain! Walking slowly makes it more effective and does more to stimulate proprioception. When a student can do this effortlessly, encourage them to walk backward with their eyes closed.

Integrating Literacy Into Physical Development Instruction and Intervention

Many of the activities that build core strength, gross motor coordination, balance, sense of self in space, and cross-lateral integration are also excellent interventions and supports for phonemic awareness, phonics, and other literacy skills. Chapters 4 and 5 will give you specifics for the following body/brain-building activities that also reinforce or support literacy skills:

❖ KaBoom!, page 79

❖ Water Paint the Walls, page 80

❖ Letter/Word Hopscotch, page 89

❖ Letter/Word Twister, page 90

❖ Musical Letter/Word Chairs, page 91

❖ Fly Away, page 91

❖ Letter/Word Blizzard Balls, page 93

Early Reading Instruction & Intervention: A Sourcebook for PreK–2 © 2013 by Cindy Middendorf • Scholastic Teaching Resources

Nurturing Physical Development Every Day

8:45 A.M. The first graders in Ms. K's class begin to dribble through the door. Because Ms. K consciously taught and practiced routines and procedures during the first several weeks of school, children know exactly what to do when they enter the classroom. Ms. K and the children think of it as "morganizing" (getting their brains, bodies, and materials ready to begin the school morning). Ms. K knows that the predictable, purposeful routine each day offers children a sense of independence, builds core strength, allows cross-lateral practice, reinforces eye-hand integration, and nurtures literacy skills.

After being greeted by Ms. K at the door, Ellie and Sanja, have already deposited their take-home folders in the appropriate basket, settled their things into the closet, and dragged their pictures on the whiteboard into the appropriate column for their respective lunch choices. Both now head toward the Brain-Building Wall. Ellie chooses to stand on the footprints that are on the floor in front of the Circle Circuit, while Sanja goes to the Push-Up Place and stands patiently behind Cory, who is completing push-ups. "Hey, look at me," boasts Cory. "I'm standing behind the footprints, and it's still easy for me. Back, up, Sanja." Cory pushes off the wall, keeping his back straight, just as he's been taught. As he pushes, he recites the months of the year and then the days of the week. Each week Ms. K posts a different brain builder that engages children while they exercise. Sometimes they start at a given number and count by twos, fives, or tens to a target number. Sometimes they say and spell three or four words from the spelling list posted on the wall by the Push-Up Place. Occasionally they have to sing a verse of a favorite class song or pretend they are telling a story to the wall.

9:00 A.M. All of Ms. K's first graders have arrived, been greeted, signed in for lunch, and completed their brain builders at the wall. Ms. K knows that for Jeremy, the push-ups every morning are an important intervention for his very weak trunk muscles. She realizes that for Kandace, the push-ups simply maintain the adequate core strength she already exhibits, and that for Paulie, the push-ups allow him to show off his strength every day! Likewise, Ms. K knows that Thomas doesn't really need the Circle Circuits every day, but the exercise is good for him, and that it is a crucial intervention for Lara, who is still struggling with comfortably crossing the midline.

Ms. K strums her xylophone, giving the two-minute warning. Children are now scattered, engaged in the early-morning, free-choice center activities. Some are in the Book Nook, several are at the Free Writing Center, four are at the Listening Center, and others are standing—and sitting—in front of the whiteboard where a slide show of last week's Fruit Fest is running. Although children have seen the slide show on the last four mornings, they never tire of reading the text they wrote that appears with the slides. They giggle at the pictures of themselves and their friends. Upon hearing the xylophone, Jaime, this week's Technology Expert, comes forward and shuts down the slide show. Within two minutes, each child is standing behind his or her chair, and this week's Flag Holder is in front of the class with the flag.

Ms. K announces (as she does every day), "Straight and tall, shoulders back, feet together, right hands in place. Let's pledge our promise to our country."

Ms. K knows that the simple body control required to stand straight with shoulders back and feet together requires core strength and balance, both important building blocks for literacy readiness.

Everyone recites the Pledge of Allegiance, sings the Patriotic Song of the Month, and the day begins.

Instructional Interventions and Supports During Transition Times

Use every opportunity available to strengthen the core, balance, and muscle integration of your young learners. Use the 15, 30, or 60 seconds that are wasted while children are lining up or waiting in line. You can easily slip in instructional practice and reinforcement several times a day while working on basic physical readiness. Remember, "Idle neurons are the devil's workshop!" While children are engaged in effective body builders, double the impact by using the time for skill practice also.

Most of the following transition activities involve practicing an academic skill while activating movement and incorporating brain-body interaction. All of them are valuable for energizing all children, all the time, but are especially crucial as intervention and support for those whose physical development is immature.

❖ "Stand on your tippy-tippy toes and spell your name. Now balance on your heels and spell each word I give."

❖ "Bend your arms in front of you and let each hand grab the elbow of the opposite arm. Hold your elbows and lift them over your head so that your face is in the frame. Hold that pose while we sing our 'Four Oceans' song."

❖ "Stand as straight as you can. Clasp your hands behind your neck and pull your elbows back as far as possible. Count by twos to 20 (or by ones from 32 to 50, and so on)."

❖ "Raise your hands over your head. Pull in your tummy. Hook your thumbs around each other. Now flutter your fingers like a butterfly and recite the alphabet."

❖ "As you walk to your center, touch your right elbow to your left knee, then your left elbow to your right knee. Keep alternating with every step you take." (*Note:* Start with a simpler move for younger children: Ask them to stand in one place while tapping their opposite thigh with their opposite hand, one at a time. When children can accomplish that, ask them to walk while tapping. Eventually move to the opposite elbows-opposite knees exercise.)

❖ "As you walk to the closet, pick each knee up as high as you can with each step. Count your steps."

❖ "Before you get out of your chair, put your hands on each side of the chair beside your bottom. Can you push your body up and down with your arms seven times while you name the continents?"

❖ "Stand with your feet slightly apart. Put your right fist in your right armpit, your left fist in your left armpit, and your elbows out straight. Twist from side to side without moving the lower half of your body. As I ask review questions, answer by twisting and shouting!"

❖ "Stand with your feet slightly apart. Bend forward and let your arms hang down. Hold your body still but gently swing your arms like a clock's pendulum back and forth. Count by twos to 30."

Fine Motor Development: What Do Tier I Teachers Need to Know?

It's a fact: 21st century children spend less time actively exploring the three-dimensional world than their counterparts of a generation or more ago. Increased time spent with technology, the fear of the dangers of outdoor play, and the hectic schedules and lifestyles of busy and sometimes overwhelmed young parents are only three of the factors that limit vigorous, spirited play. Typically, hand dexterity sufficient for handwriting develops sometime between the ages of 3 and 6, and refines as children actively handle toys, build with blocks, mix ingredients, dig in the dirt, catch a ball, knead clay, pour water, hang items with clothespins, roll up socks, and engage in other three-dimensional play activities. Yet many children are coming to school today with poor hand development, having spent more time playing with hand-held games or watching a screen than interacting with authentic objects of play. Research confirms what early childhood teachers know: weak fine motor skills impact handwriting as well as overall school achievement and self-esteem (Feder & Majnemer, 2007).

Forcing a child to trace letters over and over and over will not improve fine motor strength nor improve dexterity. We gain strength from the neck down and from the core outward, remember? In a perfect world, no child would be handed a pencil until (a) he or she *wanted* to hold a pencil, (b) he or she had appropriate core strength (for maintaining posture while writing) and well-developed arm strength, and (c) he or she had appropriate eye-hand coordination, hand dexterity, and all the related physical milestones in place that allow for effortless manipulation of a pencil.

Since we all function in a less than perfect world, early childhood teachers must often insist that our young children learn to write names, letters, and numbers long before they have strong and nimble small muscles. While we are still nurturing their gross motor development, we must also gently coax and strengthen the fine motor skills.

Pencils: One Size Never Fits All

You would never insist that all children in your classroom wear the same size sneaker. Nor should we insist that they should all use a standard-size pencil. Hand size, strength, and development varies as much as shoe size. Offer a variety of pencils: fat kindergarten pencils, conventional primary pencils, standard No. 2 pencils, triangular-shaped pencils, pencils with commercially-prepared grips, and pencils with teacher-made grips. Let each child find the writing tool that is most comfortable for his or her own little hand.

Simple, Effective, Teacher-Made Pencil Grips

You can customize pencils easily and inexpensively. From a discount store, purchase a bag of practice golf balls, the plastic ones with holes. With just a bit of effort, you can push a No. 2 pencil through two of the holes to create a firm grip that neatly fits into the child's palm. You can accomplish the same effect with a foam ball. Although the foam balls have the advantage of being available in varying sizes, they will not last as long.

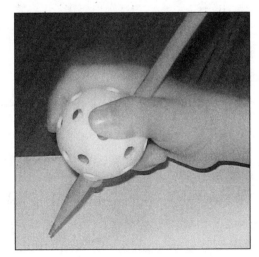

Golf Ball *A practice golf ball on a No. 2 pencil offers support and a resting place for a child's young, undeveloped hand's arch.*

Hand Sock: Is There a Correct Pencil Grip?

Although most handwriting experts agree that the tripod grip is the most efficient pencil grip, they also agree that there are acceptable variations that work equally well for many children (Le Roux, 2009). While all hands have similar physical structure, each is unique in its flexibility, size, muscle strength, and even finger webbing. The goal is for a child to hold a pencil in such a way that he or she can sustain writing neatly, with fluid movement and without hand cramps or fatigue.

Handwriting experts agree that the ring finger and pinky should be out of the way for a sustainable and productive grip, leaving the thumb, index, and middle fingers to control the writing tool. Grasping a pencil, like feeding oneself, develops in a very predictable continuum. By age 5 or 6, most children are beginning to use the mature tripod grip, but some are still using an immature "five-finger" pencil grasp, with the pinky as a stabilizer.

Use an old sock to train those little fingers how to feel the tripod grip. Children's crew socks with a 3- or 4-inch elastic band work well. Cut off the foot of the sock and cut a small hole for the thumb. Give the child a cotton ball, penny, or wadded tissue to hold against his or her palm, using only the ring and pinky fingers. Slide the hand through the sock cuff, putting the thumb in the thumb hole, index and middle fingers emerging through the foot end of the cuff, while the ring finger and pinky are holding the cotton ball against the palm. Now our writer has only thumb, index, and middle fingers free to hold the pencil.

Hand Sock *Use an old sock with the foot cut off and a hole cut for the thumb to train little fingers what it feels like to be in handwriting position.*

Binder Clips: Training Wheels for Pencil Grip

Another excellent intervention for a weak or incorrect pencil grip can be achieved using an office binder clip on a No. 2 pencil. Older children or those with chubbier fingers may need larger binder clips than young children. Place the binder clip on the pencil, about an inch from the point, with the "legs" of the clip in the up position. Now you have created a channel (the top of the clip) that is the perfect size for a small child's index finger. With the index finger in place, the thumb naturally goes below on one side and the middle finger goes on the other side.

Is a child's positioning of fingers—the grasp—on the pencil important? Yes and no. The goal of a "correct" pencil grasp is twofold: legible handwriting *and* comfort with minimal fatigue in the hand, wrist, and arm. Experts agree that the conventional tripod grasp gives the child excellent control over the pencil and also is minimally tiring for the human hand, but that other grips can be comfortable and produce legible results (Koziatek & Powell, 2002). Many children develop awkward, ineffective grasps because their hands are not yet ready for sustained writing, and in an effort to find a position that doesn't tire or cramp their hands, they become very creative with their fingers!

What to do? Certainly it is more effective to train the young hand early for an acceptable grasp than to try to correct the grasp of a third or fourth grader who resists writing because of hand fatigue. But be careful! For a child with an unconventional, established grasp, who writes legibly with no signs of hand cramping or fatigue, we can do more harm than good if we insist that he or she hold the pencil in a standard fashion. *If it isn't broken, don't fix it!*

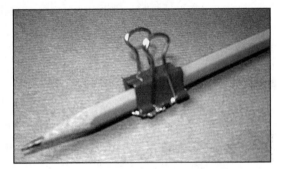

Binder Clip *This "training wheel for handwriting" allows a channel for resting the index finger. A child's thumb and middle finger will stay off the top of the pencil!*

Interventions and Supports for Fine Motor in Tier I

For our children who are right on track developmentally, specific fine motor exercises will nurture the natural progression of small muscle development. For those who are developmentally young or who exhibit red flags for learning problems, the following small muscle exercises serve as important interventions. By using ordinary, inexpensive tools, we can give these little hands and fingers daily workouts.

❖ **Spray bottles:** Take a basket of small spray bottles and one- or two-gallon jugs of water to the playground with you. Let children use a funnel to fill the spray bottles, and then ask them to "spray paint" letters, numbers, sight words, and so on, on the wall of the building or on the sidewalk.

❖ **Paper clip letters:** Ask children to make one or more paper clip chains using a specific number of paper clips. Or make it a patterning exercise by providing colored paper clips. When children have their chain(s) complete, they can shape the chains into letters, numbers, or even words (if they work with one or more partners). Keep students' fine muscles exercising by having them take the paper clip chain apart when done!

❖ **Clay with toothpicks and other tools:** Clay offers a real workout! It is stiffer, requires more muscle power, and never dries out like more pliant modeling compounds. Rolling real clay into balls and strings helps develop elasticity in the palmar arch (the "cup" in the palm), an important factor in avoiding fatigue in handwriting. Your active learners who have difficulty focusing in whole-group discussions may attend better if they're allowed to knead a ball of clay while listening. (Yes, you must teach the responsibility that comes with that privilege!) Children can make a small wall of the clay and insert colored toothpicks to create a pattern or simulate a math problem. Or ask them to press clay into a flat "slate" and use a toothpick (or crochet hook or pencil) to write letters, practice sight words, do number problems, draw figures, or trace shapes into the surface For more fun (and learning), ask children to use scissors and cut out shapes from clay.

❖ **Pom-poms, tweezers, and tongs cleanup:** Want some fun at the end of the day? Or do you just need to offer Jonah an outlet for all his energy? Hand out large pom-poms, tweezers, or appetizer or salad tongs (the pincer kind, *not* the scissor kind!) and declare Cleanup Time. Scraps and dust bunnies disappear from the classroom floor and little hands get a major workout! (Follow this exercise with handwashing and/or sanitizing.)

❖ **Tennis-ball talkers:** Canvass families and local tennis clubs for old tennis balls. Use a marker to draw a "mouth" along one of the existing lines on the ball. *Carefully, carefully,* cut along the mouth with scissors, a craft knife,

SEEK OUT STAFF SUPPORT

If you are fortunate enough to have an occupational therapist on staff at your school, you have a dynamic resource of knowledge and intervention strategies at your fingertips. It takes a whole village to raise a child! Pick the brains of your occupational and physical therapists, your speech and language teachers, your special ed staff, and any other resource people in your school. As a Tier 1 specialist, you will find these people excellent consultants.

or a box cutter. Cut just far enough so that you create a mouth without cutting the ball in two. You can add eyes, nose, and hair, but children love just the "tennis-ball talkers." They must squeeze the tennis ball to make the mouth "talk." With a basket of these at the Book Nook, children can have the ball "read" a book. Some children may choose to have the ball speak for them at sharing time. Or they can have the ball say and spell each spelling word or sight word.

> **TIP!**
>
> Drawing a smiley face on the left end of the paintsticks or dowels will give children a visual starting point. Tell students, "If the smiley face is right side up, you're starting at the right end!"

❖ **Clothespins and paintsticks or dowels:** Spring-type wooden clothespins make small hands work hard (and they're inexpensive!). Write letters or numbers on the clothespins and separate them into cups, berry baskets, frosting tubs, or half-pint milk cartons that have been labeled, so children can easily find the clothespins they need. (You don't need a separate container for each letter; put all lowercase and uppercase *A*s, *B*s, and *C*s in one; *D*s, *E*s, and *F*s in another; and so on. Finding letters quickly allows more time on task, and less time looking for the right clothespin!) PreK children can clip clothespins that spell their name, or clip numbers in sequence; kindergarten children can practice word families; first graders can clip on sight words; second graders can practice spelling words. Or use a longer dowel and let students write sentences. Have paper nearby so they can record what they have written on the paintstick or dowel.

❖ **Turkey basters and cotton balls:** For lots of indoor recess fun, clear off a long table or pathway on the floor for Air Races! Give two children each a turkey baster and a cotton ball. Mark a starting line and a finish line. Children must move the cotton ball using only the puffs of air from the turkey baster. Using colored cotton balls helps keep it obvious who is in the lead.

❖ **More pom-poms and tweezers:** Thoroughly wash several 12- and 16-ounce plastic juice bottles of varying shapes, both wide-necked and narrow-necked. Put a letter, number, or shape on each bottle so it can be identified. Gather an assortment of tweezers in varying sizes. Ask children to use the tweezers to put pom-poms (or buttons, macaroni, or other fillers) into the plastic bottles. You could spell words together, and students could deposit one pom-pom for each letter, or you could count by twos or fives, putting in one pom-pom for each number, or you could just let them put in as many as they can in a set time. You could add a recording sheet and have children write their estimate of how many pom-poms they will use to fill a bottle. After students fill the bottle, they must empty it and count the contents. They can make piles of tens to check the estimation.

❖ **Spinning jacks:** Another great indoor recess activity! Give each child a smooth tray or burner cover with edges that will keep the jacks from escaping. Provide both large and small metal and plastic jacks. Teach children to use their index finger and thumb to spin a jack on one of its legs. When they get good at it, challenge them to spin one jack with each hand at the same time.

❖ **Jar lids and zippered plastic bag:** Whenever you store manipulatives in a jar or zippered plastic bag, children must use important small muscles to open them. The exercise is doubled when students return the objects to the jar or bag and close it!

❖ **Sign language:** Teach children (and yourself!) to sign the alphabet, color words, and simple courtesies ("please," "thank you"). This not only gives the hand a workout in dexterity and flexibility, but also allows another modality— finger spelling—for teaching letters and spelling words.

With children, learn and practice a letter at a time, along with one or two simple phrases, colors, or numbers. Not all children will have the finger dexterity to sign fluently, but this powerful second language will exercise those muscles, offer another avenue for learning, and enrich their world.

SIGNING MADE EASY

Several Web sites can help you teach yourself to sign the alphabet. Do a search for American Sign Language, or go directly to any of these sites:

- aslpro.com
- lifeprint.com
- aslbrowser.comtechlab.msu.edu/ browser.htm

The popular children's literacy Web site Starfall.com also has a kid-friendly sign-language alphabet. Just go to "Main Index" and click on the two hands in the lower left corner. Then click on any letter to hear the letter name and see the sign for it.

CHAPTER 2

Interventions Within Whole-Group Instruction

A very wise special ed teacher once said to me, "If all teachers from preK through second grade would teach using only special ed strategies, we'd have fewer third-grade kids identified as special ed!" Her insight, ahead of the research, validates what most early childhood teachers know: commonsense, brain-based strategies that are specifically aimed at at-risk learners are the most powerfully effective strategies for *all* children. All children need special education when "special" means giving each the tools, supports, and approaches that best support his or her learning.

Research on modalities of learning, multiple intelligences, the relationship between emotions and learning, and the uniqueness of the brain confirm that *all* children, not just at-risk or special needs children, but *all* children benefit from differentiated strategies (Marzano, Pickering, & Pollock, 2001). As Tier 1 intervention specialists, we must make certain that our whole-group strategies give the biggest bang for our instructional buck for both competent and at-risk students. How can we engage more of the children more of the time?

> A teacher should keep in mind two things. First, the subject matter must be within the range of the child's interests and experience. . . . Second, to reach the desired results, the children must be in a responsive attitude toward the teacher. A good understanding between teacher and pupil is an absolute necessity before the former can lead where she wills. This once established, the children will follow in almost any pathway.
>
> —from *Practical Methods, Aids and Devices for Teachers* by Walter J. Beecher & Grace B. Faxon, Volume 1, 1916

Teacher Talk: What Do Teachers Need to Know?

The average child in our early childhood classrooms processes (hears and understands) speech at the rate of about 120–125 words per minute, but the average teacher speaks at the rate of 145–160 words per minute (Hull, 2010). Simply slowing our speech down, articulating and enunciating correctly, will increase aural comprehension. I am certainly not suggesting that teachers resort to "snail talk," nor could I ever personally maintain the pace of speech that brought fame to the beloved Fred Rogers (of *Mister Rogers' Neighborhood*). But we need to be consciously aware of the danger of speaking too rapidly, especially for at-risk learners. Could it be that when we chastise a class with, "You're not listening!" that our children's young brains are pleading, "We *are* listening; we're just not listening fast enough!" The research of Hull and others consistently points out that children cannot process information as quickly as teachers often dispense it.

The second "teacher talk" issue that we must be aware of is the amount of time children spend listening to *us*. Fact: The voice heard most often in an early childhood classroom is the teacher's. While no one disputes the need for teacher direction, encouragement, and instruction, researchers confirm that talking anchors learning and that the one who is talking (discussing, debating, questioning, thinking out loud) about the topic at hand is the one whose brain is most actively engaged in learning (Jensen, 2005).

Consciously monitor yourself in your classroom, and ask:

❖ Is it always necessary to repeat directions two or three times? When we regularly repeat, children learn that it's OK not to listen the first time, since there will always be another chance. A better strategy is to have students "ask a friend who was listening."

❖ Is it always necessary to rephrase or repeat a child's answer so that the class hears *my* answer, not the child's? Could we be teaching children that their answer is good, but not good enough? Does rephrasing make children think the following: *If Ms. K is going to repeat what my classmates say, why should I focus on them while they are speaking? And if Ms. K is going to repeat what I say, why do I need to speak clearly to my classmates?*

❖ Is it always necessary to comment after each answer a child gives? Could we be teaching children that every answer needs a comment (most often, a teacher affirmation)? When an answer is appropriate, model nonverbal, positive feedback with a smile and a nod and then move on.

When I consciously tracked my own teacher talk in my own classroom, I was chagrined to realize how often I spoke when it wasn't really necessary. I noticed that during whole-group time, when a child answered one of my open-ended questions, all eyes would turn to me to see what I had to say about the answer, as though I alone could deem the response worthy. When I started simply giving thoughtful looks, nodding, scratching my head, or furrowing my eyebrows, children were at first confused as they waited (not always patiently!) for one of my traditional pronouncements: "Good thinking!" or "Great point!" or "Are you sure about that?" or "Let's think about that!" Yes, it's important that we encourage and nurture with our words, but excessive affirmation often rings hollow—even to the ears of a child.

Teach and model active listening, and make it natural for children to actively listen and to comment on one another's thoughts. I know from experience that even rowdy kindergarten children from homes where there is little modeling of courteous behavior can be taught to respectfully disagree, to listen to their peers, and to defend their own thinking.

Tier 1 Strategies for Whole-Group Instruction: Learning to Listen

At any given moment in any given elementary school, chances are good that a child or group of children are hearing these words: "You need to listen more carefully!" or "Put on your listening ears!" or "You're NOT listening!" I've said them myself.

Hearing is a passive behavior, but listening involves active attention and processing. We hear when sound waves are funneled into the outer ear, vibrate the eardrum, and send messages to the auditory cortex of the brain through the intricate interplay of tiny bones and fluid. When we listen, those sound waves are translated into meaningful auditory stimuli. That requires several other areas of the brain to be engaged. Hearing comes naturally; listening must be taught, modeled, and practiced. The children most in need of intervention are often those with the poorest listening skills. Integrate active listening into every aspect of the learner's day:

❖ Teach children what listening looks like and feels like, and encourage them to practice the posture, eye contact, and mental engagement involved. Copy, enlarge, and post the I Am a Good Listener poster on page 140.

❖ Turn a read-aloud into active listening by giving children a purpose for listening. List three or four points they need to listen for especially: *"As you listen to* Mufaro's Beautiful Daughters, *I know you'll enjoy the award-winning illustrations. Be sure to listen for the answers to these questions: Why was Manyara always in such a bad mood? Why didn't Nyasha tell her father about the way her sister treated her? What sound did Manyara hear that told her the city was very near?"* Giving listeners a purpose is not simply a good intervention for those who struggle with comprehension; it also strengthens active listening skills for all children.

❖ Use the Partner Repeats strategy on page 43 to build the habit of actively listening to peers.

❖ Model active listening. When a child speaks to us—during class discussion or in casual conversation—we need to look at him or her and genuinely listen to the words and the feelings behind them. Every child deserves to know that you've *listened,* but feedback doesn't always need to be verbal. You can validate a child's comments with eye contact and a facial expression like a nod and a smile or a furrowed brow and a concerned pat on the shoulder.

Wait Time/Processing Time

Simply waiting longer between asking a question and allowing an answer can be a powerful intervention for some students. Sound too simple? Consider a simple, recall question with a one-word answer like, "What day is the day after tomorrow?" Let's look at the internal dialogue happening inside the minds of several students:

Anastasia: *(thinking to herself)* Simple. It's Thursday. *She eagerly shoots her hand into the air and waves her arm.*

Carlos: *(thinking to himself)* Um, today is Tuesday, so there's Wednesday, then Thursday. *He raises his hand.*

Bradley: *(thinking to himself)* Uh, let's see. Oh, I know. The days are on the calendar. Where's the calendar? Oh, there it is, on that wall. Um. Let me look. Um. OK, today is, um, let me see, um, Tuesday. So let's see . . . I know the days of the week, um, Sunday, Monday, Tuesday, Wednesday,

Early Reading Instruction & Intervention: A Sourcebook for PreK–2 © 2013 by Cindy Middendorf • Scholastic Teaching Resources

Thursday, yeah, it's Thursday. *His hand goes up.*

Maria: *(thinking to herself)* I don't know, but I want to look smart, so I'll raise my hand. If she calls on me, I'll just say, "I forgot."

Andre: *(thinking to himself)* Thursday, I think. But maybe that's not right. I could be wrong. I just won't raise my hand.

Stacey: *(thinking to herself)* I don't know. I can't wait for lunch. I hope Mama put strawberry jam on my sandwich and not grape jelly.

Yes! You recognize those students! Average wait time in a classroom is one second or less (Cotton, 1988), and we typically call on one of the first three hands that shoots into the air. One second! That means that before Bradley has even processed the question, Anastasia or another quick thinker, with arm waving in the air, has been called upon to give the answer. In reality, Bradley will not even bother to finish his thinking once the answer is given. What are we teaching Bradley? And obviously Stacey learned long ago that she'll never figure out the answer in time to raise her arm and get called on.

Consciously wait at least three or four seconds after you ask a question before you invite a child to answer. For questions that require a deeper level of thought, increase the wait time. Experts (Rowe, 1987; Stahl, 1990) tell us that when teachers lengthened wait time to between three and five seconds, the following positive changes occurred:

❖ the length of responses increased for questions that were not one-word answers

❖ the number of correct/appropriate responses increased

❖ the number of "I don't know," and "I forgot" responses decreased

❖ student retention of material improved

Increased wait time, an intervention for students who process more slowly, encourages richer thinking for all students. When you are posing questions to the class, keep Bradley in mind!

Choral Answers

Teach children that you will often ask a question that requires a choral answer, that is, all children will answer at once. Tell them that if they fear the answer will "sneak out of your mouth" prematurely, they can actually use one hand to cover their mouth or to pinch their lips together. (My class called this "Duck Lips!") The cue is, "On the count of three, answer me." After an appropriate wait time, say, "One, two, three," and let every child with an answer say it. This strategy works best for simple questions that have only one or two correct answers.

Turn and Talk

The fact that *talking anchors learning* bears repeating: The more learners verbally echo information, the more they discuss a topic, and the more they repeat pertinent facts, the better they will master the material. For many students, talking simply reinforces the learning they have already mastered. For others, talking is the intervention that will cement the learning in their brains.

Divide your class into "talking teams" of two or three children for whole-group discussion time. Call them listening partners, learning partners, study buddies, or any other term that indicates the expectation of helping, supporting, and cooperating. In a perfect world, children would be allowed to choose their own teammate(s), but somehow, my classroom worlds have never been perfect. I found that I could sometimes allow students to choose their own talking buddies, but more often, to foster rich learning and discussion, I have had to assign partners. I would switch partners often, especially as the class became a more cohesive unit, and children quickly understood that they were expected to help everyone all the time.

CHORAL ANSWERS: AN INTERVENTION STRATEGY

Suppose you said, "On the count of three, answer me (pause)" and ask this question: "What is the brain's number one, most important need?" Allow a 3-second wait time and then say, "One, two, three." What happens in your classroom? Nolan, who knows the answer instantly, gets to proudly and confidently declare, "Oxygen!" At the same time, Lilly, thinking she knows the answer, but having little confidence, quietly whispers, "Oxygen?" and listens to see if her answer matches the louder answers. Max says, "Water!" and gets immediate feedback for his misinformation when he hears the choral response, "Oxygen." Teresa, who hasn't a clue about the answer, hears it loudly and clearly from several different directions. Choral answers invite everyone to be engaged and on task!

Occasionally during whole-group discussion or instruction, ask a question and tell students to "turn to your talking buddy and agree on an answer." Or instruct them to "find out what your talking buddy thinks the boy in the story should have done," or "see if your talking buddy can remember four characteristics that make an animal a mammal." Then give children a minute or so to discuss, answer, and listen to one another.

If a team is obviously at a loss, ask another team to share their thoughts with them. After the allotted time, ask one or more teams to answer, then turn the partner discussions into a whole-group discussion.

Partner Repeats

An extension of Turn and Talk is Partner Repeats. In this powerful strategy, the talking partners must listen carefully to each other because they may be asked to repeat, in their own words, what their partner said. Even very young children learn quickly that they must listen, since they will likely be asked to share their partner's thoughts. Our competent learners expand their understanding by considering others' views (and sometimes correcting their partner's misconceptions). Our at-risk learners need a multitude of opportunities to listen and rephrase what they have heard and to consider the input of others.

When teaching this strategy, start simply with questions like, "Find out what food your talking partner likes best for breakfast," or "Ask your partner to tell you something he or she is really good at." Once children are confident with this strategy, use it to reinforce learning: "Turn to your partner and ask him to name three mammals, different than the three that you name." Incorporate this strategy into opportunities for higher-order thinking: "Ask your partner how he or she would change the ending of the story," or "Find out what other stories your partner is reminded of when we read this story."

In Your Own Words

You've read it before: talking anchors learning, especially for auditory learners. Verbalizing when learning helps us focus on the task, retain the information, and engage another neural pathway (Schunk, 1986).

Teach children to rephrase a classmate's comments. They soon learn to listen to their peers when they know they may be asked to put a peer's answer into their own words. This strategy is very similar to Partner Repeat, but it involves actively listening during whole-group instruction. A typical example of this strategy follows:

Deena: I think it doesn't matter whether you put the three buttons down first or the four because either way it makes seven buttons.

Teacher: Hmmm . . . Charlie, put Deena's thoughts into your own words.

Charlie: Well, she said kinda like that if you add three and four it's the same as if you add four and three 'cause they add up to seven.

Or consider this exchange during a science lesson:

Teacher: How are reptiles and mammals alike?

Gina: They all have a backbone.

Teacher (*nodding*): Issac, would you please say Gina's answer in your own words?

Issac: Well, that's not what I was thinking, but she said that snakes and lizards and all the reptiles have a backbone, um, a spine, just like mammals have a spine.

Talking Anchors Learning

Ms. K is in her "comfy chair" with students seated in two large semicircles on the rug. She knows that this seating arrangement allows them to pay better attention to each other during whole-group discussion, including making eye contact and reading facial expressions. Students are becoming adept at using the whole-group learning strategies that Ms. K has modeled, encouraged, and reinforced for weeks.

It's early November. Ms. K and her class have just finished a unit on the five senses, as well as learning about changes in nature and human behavior brought on by the shift from autumn into winter. Today Ms. K plans to facilitate a discussion that will make children aware of seasonal elements that affect our senses.

She and her students have created a chart on the easel titled "Our Senses in the Fall." Under the title are five columns labeled, "I Hear," "I See," "I Smell," "I Taste," and "I Touch." Children helped share the pen with Ms. K to write the title and the headings.

Ms. K: Put on your duck lips! *(Some children pinch their lips together, others visibly lock their lips.)* On the count of three, tell me another name for the season we call fall. *(Ms. K raises her eyebrows and looks around expectantly for about three seconds.)* One, two, three . . .

Students: Autumn!

Ms. K: Well, let's get caught on thought about autumn! *(Some children close their eyes; some put on pretend thinking caps; some massage their temples. They've learned that "caught on thought" means that they all must, in their own way, focus their brain on one idea or topic for several seconds. They know that when Ms. K announces "caught on thought," a question will follow that could have lots of "right" answers.)*

Ms. K: I can see you're ready to think. Here's the thought: How many ways can you think of that our senses help us think that this season is autumn? Ready? Think!

(The room is quiet for 30 seconds. Students know that hands-in-the-air are not allowed yet, and that even Ms. K appears to be thinking deeply.)

Ms. K: OK, turn and talk. *(At this prompt, all children turn to one or two others near them to discuss their thoughts. These turn-and-talk partners have been preassigned—with much thought—and change periodically throughout the year when Ms. K changes* *seating on the rug. Like all effective early childhood teachers, Ms. K is skilled at honing in on bits and pieces of several ongoing conversations. After 60 seconds, Ms. K gives one blow on her train whistle. Children know that is the cue for wrapping up their peer talk, and they are eager for the next step.)*

Ms. K: Let's see how well you considered each other's ideas. Shelley, tell us one thing your talking partner said about how her senses tell her it's autumn.

Shelley: *(smiling at Leah, sitting beside her)* Well, Leah says her Papa and Grammy have a fireplace, and when she gets to their house, she can smell it burning from outside, and then she knows it's fall 'cause the fireplace smoke is what she smells.

When Shelly finishes speaking, Ms. K looks at Leah with an expectant look, waiting for Leah's comment.

Leah: *(a girl of few words!)* Yeah, that's what I said.

Without comment, Ms. K quickly writes "fireplace smoke" under the heading "I Smell" on the chart. Later (or on another day), she will use this chart for literacy instruction. Even now, as she writes, several children are whispering "fireplace smoke."

Ms. K: Anyone else ready to share what they heard their talking partner say?

Several hands shoot up, as grinning children look at their partners.

Ms. K: Issac? *(Issac and all the children know they are each responsible for being able to retell what their talking partner said, even though not everyone will be asked.)*

Issac: I got Toby and Rosa here, and Toby says in the fall he sees leaves of all colors. So that's sense of sight, and I said that, too, and so did Rosa. We all see all the leaves, but we see them fall, too, so that's seeing, too, huh? And that rhymes, huh? We all see them fall.

Ms. K smiles, nods approvingly, and jots down "colorful leaves" and "falling leaves" under the heading "I See." Ms. K points to Sarajane.

Sarajane: Gary says you see snow and that makes it fall, but I said no, 'cause snow is a winter thing.

Ms. K *(looking interested):* Hmmm . . . What do you think about that, boys and girls? *(She nods toward Michael.)*

Michael: I know that it can snow in the fall sometimes, just those little flecks of snow.

Gary: *(interrupting)* That's what I meant, but I said "flakes," Michael, not "flecks."

Several children giggle, and someone offers, "Snowflecks, that's silly."

Ms. K: *(with a grin)* Actually, flecks are tiny pieces of something, so *snowflecks* isn't such a crazy word! So, boys and girls, turn to your talking partner and see what you think about snowflakes, or snowflecks, being seen in the autumn. *(She listens for about 30 seconds as the circle buzzes with chatter about snow in the fall, and then she gives a quick train whistle.)*

Ms. K: Thumbs up or thumbs down? We can sometimes see and feel snowflakes in the fall. *(Most children eagerly put their thumbs in the air. They've learned that this is a quick and quiet way to agree or disagree with a statement. Joelle puts her thumbs down until she looks around, receives instant feedback, and quickly corrects her learning. Without comment, Ms. K writes and reads "snowflakes" under the heading "I See.")*

Ms. K: What about other senses that tell us it's fall? Tell us your ideas or your talking partner's ideas. Barry?

Barry: Jessie said you can hear leaves making noises.

Ms. K: What do you mean by that, Jessie?

Jessie: I can hear leaves when they're all dried up, and I kick them into a pile, and they sound all crunchy and crackly.

Ms. K gives a wink and a thumb-up, quickly writes and reads "leaves crunching" under "I Hear." She points to Nania.

Nania: Well, the leaves make a noise if the wind blows really hard and knocks them all around, too, but I want to use the sense of taste because fall is when we get to eat candy apples!

Ms. K: *(pointing to Vickie)* Nania's idea in your words, Vickie?

Vickie: She likes eating apples, candy apples.

And so it goes. Like a maestro, Ms. K has orchestrated the conversation to include interventions (extra thinking time, student clarification of other's thoughts, peer teaching) that are crucial for her at-risk students. She will use the chart produced during the whole-group discussion for follow-up literacy instruction later in the week.

CHAPTER 3

Tools for Best Practice and Interventions

Our colleagues in 1916 knew that no one strategy, tool, or tip is a one-size-fits-all answer to helping every child grow and succeed. Like teachers then, we endeavor to have all children paying attention, being engaged, processing thought, and embedding learning.

What Do Tier 1 Teachers Need to Know About Classroom Tools and Supports?

"The class is full of individual needs, and for each individual you must have a separate ideal. Oh, yes, you will have to work, and you will have to think. There are no set rules to go by. Nothing is cut and dried. It demands constant watchfulness, constant alertness, and the expenditure of enthusiasm and magnetism."

—from *Practical Methods, Aids and Devices for Teachers* by Walter J. Beecher & Grace B. Faxon, Volume 1, 1916

In a classroom of 25 children, there are 25 unique ways of neural processing, 25 different combinations of modalities and intelligences, and 25 personalities, each with loveable (or not so loveable!) quirks. We have neither the time nor the neurological training to explicitly assess, diagnose, and prescribe the perfect learning conditions for each individual. Even if we could, where would the time and resources come from to accommodate them all?

Twenty-five competent cooks in a kitchen would have 25 different preferences for the combinations of pots, knives, chopping utensils, and spices necessary to guarantee successful meals. Some will do better with an apron on; for others, it makes no difference. Some need the printed recipe in front of them; others can read it once and proceed without any further reference to it. Some will ask for very precise measuring cups; others will eyeball amounts. Yet all could potentially prepare an award-winning meal. Rather than assign standard pots, knives, cutting boards, and measuring tools to each chef, it would make more sense to provide a reasonable variety of tools and allow each cook to settle on the ones that work for him or her.

The young "cooks" in our classroom are just beginning to develop their unique thought processes and work habits. Doesn't it make sense to offer them a variety of "utensils" and allow them to explore and ultimately settle on the ones that work with their own learning preferences? I rarely use the pineapple corer in my kitchen, but knowing that it is available makes me more likely to tackle the recipe that calls for fresh pineapple.

Which tools are most likely to help children focus, work independently, improve handwriting, and listen? Thank goodness that brain researchers have done much of the work for us. What we know about the workings of the brain in early childhood learners is still minimal compared with all there is to know. Yet research has given us enough ground rules so that we are able to competently offer the tools that can provide intervention for our struggling learners and promote engagement for all learners.

Not surprisingly, many Tier 1 interventions involve tools and devices that special education teachers, as well as occupational and physical therapists, have been using for years.

Strategies formerly limited to the realm of special ed are now being accepted as sound instructional support for all students. Many of the tools discussed in this chapter can be purchased from stores and Web sites that specialize in adaptive devices, but you can easily make a class set of most tools with the purchase of a few inexpensive materials.

Classroom Tools for Interventions and Support

Children may choose to use specific tools for a variety of reasons. Because every brain has its own intricate and unique neurological wiring, every child may be impacted differently when using a tool. The chart on the next page lists several intervention/engagement tools and the many benefits of each.

Intervention / Engagement Tools

	Self Management	Auditory Support	Engagement/ Attention	Handwriting Support	Reading/Writing Support
Fidgets	x		x		
Headphones	x	x	x		x
Personal Timers	x		x		
Velcro® Strips	x		x		
Chair Bands	x		x		
Whisper Phones		x	x		x
Lowercase Keyboard Covers	x				x
Page Protectors			x	x	
Highlighting Tape			x		x
Colored Overlays			x		x
Reference Folders	x			x	x
Graph Paper				x	x
Defined Workspace	x		x		

Fidgets: Keep My Fingers Busy

Materials: a variety of objects that children can handle, basket

During whole-group instruction, Erin is unraveling a thread from her sweater, twisting her ponytail, playing with the hem of her shirt, or ripping the Velcro® on her sneaker. She has to be touching something every minute, and it's driving you—and some of her classmates—crazy!

Many children—at-risk learners and many others—can truly focus better if they have something in their hands. For those children (and adults!), tactile involvement actually enhances cognition. A fidget is anything a child can have in his or her hands that can be kneaded, stroked, squeezed, rubbed, or otherwise handled in a quiet manner. Keep these objects in a basket for easy access as children gather for whole-group lessons.

Fidgets are not toys—they are tools! But, for all their research-proven value, fidgets can become a management nightmare unless you establish parameters from the very beginning. I found that the following works well:

> FIDGETS: NOT FOR CHILDREN ONLY
>
> Don't think of a fidget as being a children's tool only. Next time you are at a workshop, religious service, theater, or other gathering where adults are focusing on a speaker, make note of the "adult fidgets." Some adults doodle and sketch, some fold and unfold a program, some play with their rings or watches, some button and unbutton, some twist pen caps. Many adults need to fidget for the same reason that children do: tactile involvement helps focus attention.

> *"Girls and boys, people who study how our brains work have found that some brains work better if the person's fingers are busy. Sounds crazy, doesn't it? But it's true. For some of us, when our fingers are moving, our brain is able to pay better attention. It's called fidgeting. I have this basket of fidgets, and if you think a fidget will help you focus and learn when we are together on the rug, you're welcome to take one. There are three rules.*

> *One, if I can tell that you're paying attention to the fidget and not the lesson, you'll lose the privilege of having the fidget.*

Two, if you are using the fidget in a way that distracts classmates from learning or distracts me from teaching, you will lose the privilege.

Three, if you are using the fidget in an unsafe or unhealthy way, you will lose the privilege."

In the beginning, give children a minute to simply explore the fidgets. Then, firmly enforce the rules. Should fidgets be allowed for only the fidgety children? There are times when we must explain that some classroom tools are only for specific children. However, I have found that if I allow free choice of fidgets, eventually only children who truly need that stimulation consistently take one from the basket.

Headphones: Blocking Out the World

Materials: old sets of headphones with wires cut off, basket

Do you have an Adam in your classroom? Adam is the one who regularly approaches you with the "poor me" look: "I can't think because Jerome is humming" (or reading out loud, breathing too loud, rolling his pencil, tapping his foot). Traditional, predifferentiated classroom strategy would have us asking Jerome to control the distracting behavior. Thanks to brain imaging and neuro-research that helps us understand what is happening in a brain at any given moment, we now know that Jerome's behavior might well be helping him think better. Of course, there's always the possibility that Jerome is purposely distracting Adam. Only you know the internal classroom dynamics!

In either case, Adam needs to be able to muffle, mute, or soften the auditory distraction. Gather as many old sets of headphones as you can find. Cut off the wires, and allow children to use them whenever they need to block out peripheral noise. Although the headphones will not eliminate all background noise, most

---

FIDGETS THAT WORK

A fidget must be small, pliable, and durable enough to withstand lots of kneading, squeezing, and twisting. I've found these items work well:

- a strip of satin ribbon, about 1½ inches wide and 8 inches long
- a small squishy ball
- an old sock stuffed with cotton fluff or other old socks, tied off tightly on the end
- small stuffed animals
- a latex balloon filled with cornstarch and tied off tightly
- a sturdy ponytail scrunchie around the wrist
- a small ball of clay

Initially, I only offered one choice, so everyone who chose to use a fidget was using the same thing. A week or so later, I would offer a new set. After being introduced to one kind of fidget at a time, children eventually settled on one that worked for them.

---

children (especially strongly auditory learners who tend to hear everything) find that the surrounding sounds are muted enough to allow them to better focus.

Keep a basketful for children to use when they are working independently, or put numbers on them, and let each student keep his or hers in the desk. Be prepared! Initially, every child will think he or she needs the headphones, but eventually only those children for whom it really makes a difference will continue to use them. Intervention or quality instructional practice? Both!

Personal Timers

Materials: *a variety of timers (see sidebar for more ideas)*

Give your easily distracted students a personal sand timer to build good time-on-task habits. Before you actually use a self-management device, let students explore its qualities, play with it and predict how long it will take to empty of sand. After the initial novelty wears off, children can challenge themselves to complete a defined portion of a task before the sand runs out.

Conditioning a highly unfocused child to stay on task for one minute is a good starting place, although timers are available in 1-, 3-, and 5-minute forms. (Of course, you can also opt for the Dorothy-in-Oz version with its 60 minutes worth of sand!) Put the timer under the chair or behind

TEACHER-MADE SILENT TIMERS

You can easily assemble your own collection of personal timers with a minimum of materials and effort. These homemade timers are not precise, but they will give a child 1 or 2 minutes of time on task.

1. Collect several wide-mouthed 16-ounce juice bottles. Fill two-thirds with clear corn syrup, two or three drops of any food color, and a small handful of beads, buttons, or macaroni. Hot-glue the lid on and secure with duct tape. To use as a timer, balance the bottle on its lid. When all the beads have risen to the top, time is up. Now, flip it over to set it upright, and begin the timing again. The time required for all the beads to rise to the top will never be exactly the same.

2. From a discount store (or from an online source), purchase several glitter water batons. Make a holder for the upright baton out of a ball of clay. Flatten the bottom of the clay so that the baton will sit without tipping. Push the baton into the clay pedestal. When the glitter in the baton has reached the top, time is up! Flip the baton over, reinsert into the clay, and begin again!

the child, and challenge the child to attend to a task long enough so that when he or she checks the timer, the sand is gone. It's not about "beating" the timer. It's about working longer than the timer does. It takes practice!

Timers today have evolved from the standard hourglass design to an array of unique, engaging tools. Check teacher-supply catalogs and on-line timer sites to find liquid motion timers, timers with microbeads that flow up instead of down, and gravity glass timers.

Don't discount the value of good old-fashioned kitchen timers (also available in fun shapes, sizes, and motifs). However, I found that the timers that signal "time's up!" with a ding, a ring, or a beep became less personal and more for the community at large.

Velcro® Strips: Without the Noise

Materials: strips of Velcro®

Like all early childhood teachers, I view Velcro® sneakers as a necessary evil. I give daily thanks that the magic of Velcro® allows Georgie to go from snowboots to sneakers in less than two minutes. Yet, will students ever learn to tie laces if they are always using Velcro®? And Velcro® sneakers as a musical instrument drive us crazy! The annoying rip-rip-rip can cause even the most unflappable among us to weep and gnash our teeth, even as we tell ourselves that the ripping stems from the child's innate need for tactile stimulation, not a conscious effort to torture the teacher.

Fortunately, Velcro® is redeemed by the tactile sensation it provides. As previously discussed, some children actually maintain cognitive focus better when touching something. (Remember the fidgets?) Similar to a fidget, a strip or two of adhesive-backed Velcro® affixed under the table at a child's seat allows that child to discreetly enjoy tactile stimulation when seated. (Make sure not to leave one strip loose, which will invite constant ripping and sticking!)

Before you offer this intervention, you may want to privately conference with a child and allow him or her to help you decide exactly where to place the Velcro®. Or you may prefer to place Velcro® under all the desks or tables. Self-sticking Velcro® can be purchased at craft stores and discount department stores.

Early Reading Instruction & Intervention: A Sourcebook for PreK–2 © 2013 by Cindy Middendorf • Scholastic Teaching Resources

Elastic Chair Bands: A Leg Up on Restlessness

Materials: exercise resistance bands or inner tubes, pantyhose, bungee cords, knife, needle and thread (optional)

This effective intervention works best for students who are fidgety and can't sit still because it allows them to release energy while seated. Commercially sold as exercise resistance bands, these stretchy foot rests can be made using heavy-duty rubber strips cut from inner tubes, old pantyhose, or bungee cords (minus the metal hooks!). Simply tie or sew the elastic into a circle large enough to fit around the front legs of a student chair, yet tight enough to stay in place and provide resistance to active foot bouncing.

Whisper Phones: The Sound of My Own Voice

Materials: whisper phones or one-inch PVC pipe, two PVC elbows, or PVC C joints

Whisper phones (also known as phonics phones, pipe phones, and reading phones), a favorite tool for strongly auditory learners, are a means of focusing auditory attention for weak auditory learners and an effective intervention for learners struggling with phonemic awareness, decoding, and blending. These unique tools are available through most teacher-supply catalogs, but you don't need to spend a king's ransom to outfit your entire class. A trip to your local home improvement store for a length of PVC pipe (one-inch diameter fits small hands beautifully) cut into four-inch lengths, and two PVC elbows (one for each end) will enable you to assemble an entire class set quickly and inexpensively. Many home improvement stores will actually cut the PVC into lengths for you. Some charge a few pennies a cut; others do it for free. You could also use "C joints," PVC structures shaped like a C. These involve no cutting or elbow fitting but are most often available only in larger diameters.

Reading experts tell us that many students (of all ages), especially strongly auditory learners, comprehend better when they read aloud. The whisper phone allows children to hear their own voice amplified when they read to themselves, think aloud, or stretch sounds for inventive spelling. Because the sound is funneled directly to his or her own ear, and because the child is physically holding the phone, focus becomes intentional. Let children experiment with using these when they read to themselves, write independently at centers, and even in guided reading lessons. Expand the use to math instruction. When learning basic facts, many children will benefit from "reading" the facts to themselves over and over. Put the whisper phones in centers where children are instructed to "count quietly, to yourself."

You might not be able to distinguish the children for whom this added auditory tool is an intervention from those who simply like the idea of hearing their own voice. Like most effective Tier 1 strategies, an intervention for one child is often simply an engaging strategy for another.

Whisper Phone *A whisper phone allows children to distinctly hear the sounds as they are said when practicing inventive spelling. In addition, a whisper phone allows a child to quietly read aloud to himself or herself.*

Lowercase Keyboard Covers

Materials: keyboard covers or one-quarter inch dot stickers and fine-point permanent pen

We could certainly devote an entire book to the many ways technology can be used for intervention and Tier 1 instruction. Keyboard covers (commercially available or teacher-made) that mark the keys with both uppercase *and* lowercase letters are an effective means of leveling the playing field for struggling learners.

PreK and kindergarten teachers often hear the despair of children, especially those lacking basic awareness of print, as they search an uppercase keyboard:

> "I can't find the 'R' for my name," laments Peter, who doesn't recognize the uppercase "R."

> "Is this the lower case 'L'?" asks Kayla, pointing to the uppercase "I."

PreK and kindergarten children often recognize an uppercase letter but not its lowercase partner, or vice versa. Many are further confused by the text format of letters like *a* and *g*. A keyboard cover that marks both types of letters helps children became more self-directed and accelerates letter recognition. This is an especially effective tool for English language learners.

An online search will lead you to several sites that offer such keyboard covers. Or, for a faster solution, simply write the uppercase and lowercase letters on small dot stickers with a fine-point, permanent pen, and place them on the keys. One-quarter inch stickers work well.

Plastic Page Protectors: A Magic Slate for Practice

Materials: clear 8-inch-by-11-inch page protectors (acetate sleeves), fine-point dry-erase marker, clean pieces of cardboard, scissors; duct tape, old clean sock, O-ring, dry-erase marker

Some of the simplest, most inexpensive tools are also some of the most productive interventions. Use clear 8-inch-by-11-inch page protectors, sometimes called acetate sleeves and sold in bundles at any discount or office supply store, to make practice more engaging, especially for the struggling learners who actively avoid paper/pencil encounters! When children must complete a practice page or a skill sheet (that will not be used for assessment purposes), allow each child to slide the paper into the protector. Equip each child with a fine point dry-erase marker, and let the practice begin! This simple strategy will provide more active and focused practice for the following:

❖ Learning to write one's name. Give each young learner a sheet with his or her name at the top. Slide the name page into the page protector and have the child trace and erase over your prewritten letters as much as necessary or use your letters as a reference for writing his or her own underneath.

❖ Handwriting practice

❖ Practicing spelling words

❖ Writing and practicing math facts

❖ Learning to draw shapes

If you lack a class set of individual whiteboards (dry-erase boards), you can make a durable set using plastic page protectors. Simply cut an 8-inch by 11-inch piece of cardboard (e.g., from a shirt box or a clean pizza box) to insert into the sleeve, slide in a piece of white paper (to cover any writing or design on

MAKE THE INTERVENTIONS MANAGEABLE!

Providing interventions like fidgets, whisper phones, page protectors, and other tools is sound instructional practice in Tier 1. However, without well-defined limits, routines, and modeling, any of these could become a management nightmare. From Day 1, lay the foundation for high expectations: *"Boys and girls, using this tool to help your learning is a privilege and with every privilege comes a responsibility. We've learned the appropriate ways to use this tool, and we've practiced how to use it to help us learn. If you choose to use it as a toy instead of as a tool, or if you choose to use it in unsafe or distracting ways, you will lose the privilege."*

True, the student who most needs the tool may be the first one to find an inappropriate way to use it. If this happens, suspension of privilege should be immediate, but temporary: *"I'm sorry you chose to use this tool in an unacceptable way. Put it back. You'll have to do this morning's lesson without it. You'll get another chance, at another time, to use it appropriately."* How many chances does a child get before the privilege is suspended permanently? Obviously, if a child misuses the intervention tool over and over, it's not an effective intervention for him or her!

the cardboard), and presto! Instant, student-friendly whiteboard! Make each one even more efficient by attaching an eraser (made of an old sock) and the dry-erase marker to it. Most page protectors come with prepunched three-ring binder holes. Simply reinforce one of those holes on both sides with duct tape and attach an old sock by using an O-ring through the sock and one of the holes of the page protector. Put the dry-erase marker into the sock, and a child now can write on his or her board as you are writing on the easel or whiteboard in front of the group. Now, instead of simply watching you write "h-o-t," and erasing the /t/ to replace it with a /p/, the learner can reproduce your work on his or her own board. Adding this extra level of engagement is an important learning support for many children.

Colored Highlighting Tape: Making Learning Stick

Materials: colored highlighting tape, 3-by-5 index cards (laminated)

All learners, but especially struggling learners, need visual reinforcement. Colored highlighting tape is an effective intervention and instructional strategy in many ways, such as the following:

❖ To locate the words or phrases in text that will answer a question

❖ To mark unfamiliar words, or text that needs more explanation

❖ To find sight words, letters, or numbers in text

❖ To note a word that could be replaced with a synonym

❖ To show where a student plans to edit a sentence, add punctuation, or replace a word.

Fact: Highlighting tape can become an expensive tool, especially for visual and tactile learners who will show you many other uses for it! Recycle and reuse the highlighting tape to minimize expense and to model smart use of resources to children. Laminate several 3-by-5 index cards (or one for each child.) On each card, affix several pieces of the tape—some long pieces, some short. To ensure that the tape will readily peel from the laminate, fold over a small end on each piece, forming a tab that will not stick to the surface. Now children can easily eyeball the size they need, use it, and return it to the card when finished. I've found that most tape strips remain usable for several months before finally drying and becoming brittle.

Colored Overlays: The Focus on Text

Materials: colored overlays (sheets of transparent colored acetate), folder, scissors

Many pediatric optometrists agree that visual perceptual distortions can impede success in learning, especially in learning to read. Some children (and adults) experience blurring or movement of letters, shadows around letters or between lines, or flickering of lines when looking at text, causing the reader to become fatigued and to avoid reading. Even a child with perfect visual acuity (20/20 vision) can still have problems with distortions and shadows. Since visual perceptual disorder can be a very subtle problem, it often goes undetected unless accompanied by other, more obvious, symptoms (e.g., complaints of glare, headaches, sore eyes). Most young children with visual perceptual disorders can't even articulate what is wrong. They just avoid reading.

For many children, processing black text on a white page is visually stressful. They may not be able to verbalize their discomfort, or even to perceive that it's not "normal." Allow children to experiment with different colored overlays. Colored overlays, available at office supply stores, are thin pieces of transparent colored acetate, usually an 8-inch-by-11-inch sheet. When placed over a page of text, the colors change the light diffusion and can make the print sharper for some children. Which colors work best? Only the reader can tell, but most experts agree that blue and yellow are usually most effective (Wilkins, 2003).

Store the overlays in a flat folder, since creases and wrinkles will defeat the purpose of eliminating distortions. Cut the overlays into various-sized strips and keep them handy at your guided reading table. Allow children to experiment in finding the color that works best for them. My experience with these colored overlays has been similar to my experience with headphones, fidgets, and whisper phones: in the beginning, everyone is convinced that their brain could work better with a colored overlay on the text, but eventually only a few children consistently chose to use them.

Reference Folders: I Know Where to Find Help!

Materials: *manila folders, library pocket, wide book tape*

All learners need to know where in the classroom they can find help. Certainly we post alphabets, number charts, color words on our walls around the classroom, but most children—and especially struggling learners—do not reach visual maturity until nearly age 8. Until then, copying from the vertical plane (the wall) to the horizontal plane (the table or desk) is often visually taxing. The quick transition required, from far vision to near vision, is also visually stressful for young children. That visual transition takes considerable neural energy—energy much better spent on learning. Creating reference folders that students can review at their seats puts less stress on the visual cortex, helps students become more self managed, and builds confidence as they learn to seek out answers independently.

Make the folders easily accessible by putting all the charts, lists, clues, and data that a child needs in a file folder. The writing folder for first grade may have a list of all sight words that will be introduced during the school year, an alphabet strip with corresponding

STUDY CARRELS

Many children will concentrate better with fewer visual distractions. Justine tried to use the reference folder as an office divider, but it toppled over easily. You can buy folding study carrels for children to use as needed (or as you mandate), or you can make simple ones from almost any appropriately sized cardboard box. Just cut the box, leaving either two or three connecting sides that will stand upright. Instant private office space! Allow children to bring a study carrel to their place if it will help them focus better. Be on the lookout for the elfish genius who just wants to be where you can't see him!

Reference Folders *Grade-appropriate reference folders for math and writing provide a self-managed tool for independent work. Make a few each year and laminate. Soon you'll have a stack on a shelf that children can easily access. After laminating, glue one or two library pockets on the outside of the lamination so that you can easily change theme words or class lists.*

pictures for each letter, a list of days of the week, and color words (written in appropriately colored font). Once you laminate the folder, attach a library pocket to the outside. You can regularly change current theme words in the library pocket. Also, on the outside of the folder (I like to put it on the back), use wide book tape to attach a class list (with student photos for younger grade reference folders). Because it is on the outside of the laminate, it can easily be changed from year to year.

A math resource folder might have the shapes and shape words, a hundreds chart, sets and numbers (0 to 12 or 0 to 20, depending upon grade level), number words, basic math symbols, and vocabulary like "is equal to =," and position words or ordinal numbers with corresponding pictures.

Start by making a few reference folders for the classroom. Or make a prototype, and allow an eager volunteer to create several more for you. Over several years, I was able to create a stack of 20-plus folders that we called our Writer's Toolboxes. About half of them were math tools. They were stored on a shelf, easily accessible to all. When working independently, children knew they could take them to their seat whenever needed. Because the folders see a lot of use, I suggest using heavy laminate.

The children in my classroom found a secondary way to use reference folders that became a self-designed intervention for some. It started with Justine, an easily distracted young lady who set the reference folder up in front of her as a divider between her and the child to her left (whom she regularly accused of "looking at my paper and laughing"). This makeshift "office" did indeed help Justine focus better when working independently.

Graph Paper: A Visual Template for Handwriting

Materials: graph-paper templates

Don't spend a fortune on buying reams of graph paper, each with a different-size grid. Create a template from the table feature on a word-processing program, or use your search engine to find one of many Web sites that offer free graph paper templates. Depending upon your purpose and the age level of your children, you can design the squares to be as large or as small as you need them to be.

You can use the graph paper as an intervention (or support) in several ways.

❖ Teach children to space their writing by teaching one letter in one space; two spaces between words.

❖ Help children line up ones and tens for vertical addition and subtraction.

❖ Let older children practice spelling words by writing them on a graph that shows the configuration of the word: tall letters, short letters, below-the-line letters. Ask them to trace the configuration. This configured writing creates a strong visual input for remembering the words. (See Configured Spelling, page 84.)

❖ Use configured writing (above) for practicing sight words.

Visually Defined Workspace: Training the Eyes to Team

Materials: felt mat, tray, egg carton lid, shoebox cover, or square of nonskid shelf liner

Vision in young, and especially in struggling, learners is predominantly three-dimensional and peripheral (Hannaford, 2007). Before age 8, most children have not yet developed strength in the eye teaming muscles necessary for processing two-dimensional black text on a white page (see "Eye Ballet," page 21). Whenever possible, we can ease the visual transition by simply providing clearly defined workspaces, workspaces that will make it more comfortable for the eyes to team for near vision.

When asking children to work with manipulatives, roll clay, count out small objects, or sort anything, give them a felt mat, a tray, an egg carton lid, a shoebox cover, a square of nonskid shelf liner, or any other "field" that will clearly delineate the work area. Just keep a stack of "workmats" handy near any area where children may need them.

LET CHILDREN IN ON THE SECRETS!

As you use any of the tools suggested for intervention and support, explain to children why you are allowing the tool to be used, and how it helps their brains think "smarter." Children certainly don't need detailed explanations of neuroscience, but basic knowledge of how the brain works can empower a child to become more self-aware. Understanding that we all learn differently, that every brain has its own way of taking in information, and that we're all smart in unique ways will help build respect and tolerance for their classmates. The bonus is this: the more one understands how his or her own brain best learns, remembers, and processes information, the more self-managed one becomes. Remind children that there are many tools in the world that help people be the best they can be: eyeglasses for better vision, braces for straighter teeth, earplugs for swimmers, special gloves for golfers. Not all athletes need a knee brace, but those who do play much better with one. Not all guitar players need a pick, but those who do can't play well without it. The tools in our classroom, like all tools and devices for athletes, can help us "improve our game."

Tools of Engagement

It's guided reading time inside Ms. K's second-grade classroom. Ms. K, seated at the back table, calls for Maxwell, Kenny, Isaiah, and Josie to join her. This is her most challenging group. These children are reading and writing below grade level.

Each child stops at the group's basket and pulls out his or her gallon-sized zippered plastic bag that holds the materials for guided reading group. All bags hold the most recently read leveled reader, one or more individual pointers, the child's personal Word Journal, and a card of highlighting tape. Isaiah slides into his seat at the guided reading table ahead of the others.

Isaiah: We reading today? *(He reaches for the "witch's finger" in his bag.)*

Ms. K: Not at the beginning of group today, Isaiah, but you'll be reading. You bet you'll be reading! *(Ms. K knows that when Isaiah is reading to himself, he will need the witch's finger on the index finger of his left hand and that Josie will have an identical one on the index finger of her right hand. Each will use it to track print in his or her reader. Ms. K knows that left-handed Isaiah needs the physical movement of the finger to help him visually track the words. She also knows that Josie doesn't really need the finger to track, but she loves the way it feels and reads better with the finger in place.*

Once the others are settled, Ms. K holds out the basket of whisper phones, indicating that each child should take one.)

Max: Is it "must" or "can" today?

Ms. K: It's a "must use the whisper phone activity," Max. *(Max gives a dramatic sigh as if to say, "I really don't need this," but takes a whisper phone from the basket.)*

Ms. K begins with a one-minute game of KaBoom! (see page 79) to reinforce several sight words that continue to give these children difficulty. She knows that using the whisper phones will help them keep their voices lower and be less distracting to the

WITCH'S FINGERS

Witch's fingers are plentiful around Halloween time. Similar to a finger puppet, a witch's finger slips easily over a child's index finger and has a long, often brightly colored, fingernail that works well as a pointer. Eraser caps for pencils also make novel finger pointers for children.

rest of the class. As soon as the game is finished, Ms. K hands each child a "magic slate" made from a page protector (see page 57), complete with a sock and dry eraser. She lets students practice with her as she separates words into syllables.

Ms. K: Write this word on your magic slate. *(On the small whiteboard that she is holding, she writes "mitten." Each child writes the word on his or her whiteboard.)*

Isaiah: I know what we're going to do. We did this yesterday. We're going to figure out the parts.

Ms. K: Your friends are nodding their heads, Isaiah. I think everybody figured out that we're going to practice syllables again.

Isaiah: Can we just do it ourselves? Just erase the first syllable?

Ms. K: *(ignoring Mr. In-Charge)* Now, read the word on the count of three: One, two, three.

All: *(in unison)* Mitten. *(Ms. K notices that Kenny waited until the others said the word before he softly mouthed it. Her heart aches for this shy wallflower with no self-confidence.)*

Ms. K: How many syllables? *(All children hold up two fingers.)*

Ms. K: I'll turn my whiteboard so you can't see what I'm doing. While I erase the second syllable of *mitten*, you do that, too, on your magic slate.

Students slide their nondominant hand into the sock and carefully erase "ten"—except Isaiah who erases "mit." Ms. K turns her whiteboard around to show only "mit" left. Isaiah gives a quick look of shock, then dismay.

Isaiah: I thought you said first syllable. *(He quickly rewrites the entire word and erases "mit.")*

Ms. K: *(ignoring the comment, but hoping that Isaiah is learning that assumptions can be traps)* Here's the next word.

Ms. K, working today on dividing two-syllable words with double consonants, goes through three more words. The last is *connect,* a word that appears in the next guided reader the group will use. Ms. K spends an additional minute checking for understanding as she has children use the word in a sentence. The entire skills-support piece of this guided reading lesson has taken less than five minutes. She is now confident that Maxwell, Josie, and Isaiah are competent in this. She makes a mental note to spend another two to three minutes with Kenny during free reading time to assess his understanding, and possibly have him cut apart and reglue a few two-syllable words with double consonants. She knows what a kinesthetic and tactile learner Kenny is. Ms. K reaches for her clipboard, never far from her side, and slaps a sticky note on it. She simply writes, "Kenny—double consonants." That brief reminder will make sure Kenny gets the quick extra boost he needs.

While Ms. K is spending 15 to 20 minutes with Kenny and his group, the rest of the children are engaged in learning stations (literacy centers, seat jobs). It is obvious that Ms. K has spent time establishing routines and procedures during independent learning time, has taught children where to find and how to use the resources available, and knows that different children need—or prefer—a choice of ways in which to support their own learning. The interaction in the classroom creates a busy hum.

Henry is in the Book Nook, reading to himself with a whisper phone. Another whisper phone is seen at the Author Center where Tristan is editing his paragraph by reading it back to himself. He stops, looking puzzled, before rereading a word or sentence. Tristan puts down the whisper phone, erases something, ponders a moment, picks up the Writer's Toolbox reference folder, and deliberately scans the list of sight words in it. He rewrites something on his paper, picks up a laminated card with reusable strips of highlighting tape stuck to it, and pulls off a one-inch piece. He shakes his head, replaces that piece of tape, and pulls off a two-inch piece. He places the highlighting tape over a phrase in his writing, picks up the whisper phone, and continues to read to himself. The highlighting tape will remind Tristan that there is a part he still wants to rework.

Working right beside Tristan in the Author Center is Kamara, wearing headphones that are missing the wires. From the first day that Ms. K introduced the purpose and correct use of the headphones, Kamara has chosen to wear them whenever she is reading or writing independently, working on a skill sheet, or working in a center without a partner. She says she wears the headphones because "I like the way they feel." Ms. K knows that any tool that is not distracting the learner, or anyone else in the room, is probably serving the learner's purpose.

Students are using other inconspicuous aids to learning. Cole is also at the Author Center, his feet resting quietly on the elastic band around the chair legs without moving. Next to him is Sunita. She too has put a band on her chair, and as she writes, her feet are rhythmically bouncing on the band. Tammy, reading in the Book Nook, is obviously engrossed in her book but is continually twisting a lock of her hair as she reads. Liam, practicing spelling words with Rosie in the Word Center, is drawing the shape of words on graph paper while Rosie scans the spelling list to see which word(s) will fit in the configuration.

Every year, Ms. K works long and hard at establishing the procedures and boundaries for independent learning time, including the choice of tools and resources. She emphasizes that all the learning tools are privileges and that with every privilege comes a responsibility. When a child takes advantage of the privilege by misusing the tool in a way that distracts himself or herself or others, Ms. K firmly reminds the child that he or she chose to use it in an irresponsible way, and therefore, at least temporarily, has lost the privilege. And yes, every year Ms. K has had to take a tool away from a student who really needed it. Typically, by the second or third chance, children learn to forsake the inappropriate behavior for the privilege (and sometimes innate need) for a tool.

CHAPTER 4

Phonological Awareness and Phonics: Best Practices and Interventions

"This is one secret of the primary teacher's success: Drill, Drill, DRILL . . . with little games that can be devised. We like to avoid monotony, yet we must drill. Nothing but persistent practice is then needed to correct many glaring defects."

—from *Practical Methods, Aids and Devices for Teachers* by Walter J. Beecher & Grace B. Faxon, Volume 1, 1916

I recently read a thought-provoking article that claimed a child internalizes a letter and its corresponding sound with automaticity only after 15,000 repetitions! That means, for example, that a child must look at the letter *d* and say or hear, "*d*—/d/, /d/,—*d*" (letter name, letter sound, letter sound, letter name)15,000 times before he or she knows it without hesitation. Although I could not find the research to support that claim, my experience with early readers gives credibility to the notion that children need thousands of experiences with a letter and its sound to really know it. But what about children who get to first or second grade and still do not have automatic recall of the sound when they see a letter? Did they have less than 15,000 opportunities to see the letter and hear the sound? Were the exposures not varied enough? Or do they simply need different kinds of opportunities?

Repeated practice with phonological awareness (specifically phonemic awareness) and phonics plays a major role in literacy instruction in the early grades, and rightly so. Volumes of evidence confirm that children who inherently comprehend the structure of language (phonological awareness) and who develop automatic recognition of letter/sound associations (phonics and phonemic awareness) have significantly better achievement in reading than children who struggle with those basic skills (Goswami, 2000). As indicated in the quotation that begins this chapter, teachers in 1916 were advised to drill, drill, and continue to drill, but with "little games" to "avoid monotony." Which interventions will engage our struggling learners as they drill while keeping the instruction relevant, effective, and most important to children, engaging?

PHONOLOGICAL AWARENESS AND PHONICS:
SEPARATE BUT EQUALLY POWERFUL PILLARS OF LITERACY

Phonological awareness is a broad term that includes the understandings of how language sounds: that a sentence can be separated into words; that words can be separated into syllables; that syllables can be separated into individual sounds (phonemes). A child who is phonologically aware can also rhyme. Researchers agree that the most important subset of phonological awareness is phonemic awareness, the ability to hear, identify, and manipulate the individual sounds in words. Phonemic awareness is a stronger predictor of literacy achievement than IQ, vocabulary, or socioeconomic status (Gillan, 2004). Phonological—and phonemic—awareness is auditory; it's all about the sounds of language.

Phonics connects the auditory to the visual. Phonics is the print representation of phonemes. Without solid phonics skills, children will struggle to become readers of meaning (Armbruster, Lehr, & Osborn, 2003).

Phonological Awareness and Phonics: What Do Tier I Teachers Need to Know?

Reading research now tells us that many struggling readers in second grade and beyond struggle because they never really mastered phonemic awareness, the most elite subskill of phonological awareness. These at-risk children have not developed the intuitive ear that allows them to hear and isolate the subtle yet distinct sounds (phonemes) of the language. Although our English alphabet has 26 letters, those letters, singly and in combination, can produce 44 distinct phonemes. To become a reader, a child must be able to hear each, and to understand how these phonemes are manipulated to produce words, sentences, and ultimately meaning.

Phonemic awareness cannot be taught with a worksheet. Repeat after me, "Phonemic awareness cannot be taught with a worksheet!" Say it one more time! Phonemic awareness is all about the individual sounds that make up a word. You can teach phonemic awareness in the dark, since children use only their sense of hearing and their voice to develop this important understanding of how language works. They must actively play with sounds, manipulate sounds, isolate and replace sounds to develop phonemic awareness.

Phonics attaches the visual representation (the letter) to the sound. Because a child who has weak phonemic-awareness skills is already at risk for reading deficits, our interventions must certainly incorporate both the sound and its letter form. The research is definitive: phonics is a non-negotiable, requisite skill (White, 2005). In the aftermath of the whole language-versus-phonics debate of the early 1990s, research has concluded what good teachers have known all along: the best reading instruction balances both approaches. Phonics is important, but it cannot be taught in isolation. Rather, phonics must be embedded within a balanced literacy program of reading and writing (IRA, 1997).

Tier 1 Best Practices and Interventions for Phonological Awareness and Phonics

Whenever possible, young children should hear and/or say the sound as they look at the letter. Instead of simply pointing out the *f* on the alphabet chart and naming it as an *f*, reinforce the learning by saying, "Yes, William, that's the *f*, /f/, /f/, *f*" (letter name, letter sound, letter sound, letter name).

Have alphabet charts posted in several areas of your classroom so that you can easily take every opportunity to direct attention to the letter when giving its sound. You'll notice that most of the intervention activities listed below combine phonemic awareness (the sound) with phonics (the letter in print.) Even in second grade, many children will benefit from having an alphabet strip attached to their desk or table writing spot. Certainly that's a non-negotiable for PreK through first grade children. If it's not possible to affix an alphabet strip, have a stack of small, laminated strips in an easily accessible place so children can take them to their writing spots.

Baby Wants a Horsie

This activity gives children practice in isolating initial phonemes. Competent students love the animated, rhythmic chant, and struggling learners need the reinforcement of hearing sounds in isolation. For a fun, two-minute energizer between lessons, allow children to stand and dramatically whine (the baby role) or be stern and stomp (the mama role).

Divide the class into two sections, a "begging baby" group and a "stern mama" group. Model (for the begging babies) how to say, very rhythmically, "Baby wants a horsie; /h/-/h/-horsie; Baby wants a horsie." Let them practice, using very pleading voices, and emphasizing the beginning sound of *horsie* in the middle of the chant.

Then ask the "stern mama" group to use their best "stern mama" voices, put one hand on their hip, shake a finger at the other group, and answer very firmly, "BUT MAMA SAYS NO!"

Immediately ask groups to switch roles, and ask the new "begging baby" group to ask for another item. You can give them a word to use, or take a suggestion from the group. If you're reinforcing one particular letter/sound combination, insist that whatever the group begs for must begin with that sound. For instance, they could ask for a melon, a moustache, a motorcycle, and a mouse if you're practicing *m* /m/. Or, if you are culminating a farm unit, you could insist that everything they ask for be related to the farm theme. Reinforce classifying by playing "Baby Wants a Horsie" with only furniture words, or community helper words, or the names of trees.

Add powerful support for your struggling learners by asking a classmate to stand at the alphabet chart with a pointer during the activity. As each new word is named, the Letter Finder at the alphabet chart will point to the letter being isolated.

Silly Singing

Like "Baby Wants a Horsie," this activity delights competent students with rich and fun reinforcement while engaging struggling learners in solid instruction and intervention for phonemic awareness and phonics. Several popular children's songs become the anchor for fun phonemic awareness and phonics support. Use Silly Singing during transition times, as a warm-up for whole-group instruction, or as an afternoon energizer!

❖ Build phonemic awareness and phonics with "Old MacDonald."

Old MacDonald had a farm, E-I-E-I-O

And on this farm he had a B (Show or have your Letter Finder of the week point out the *B.*)

Be-Bi-Be-Bi-Bo

With a /b/, /b/ here and a /b/, /b/ there

Here a /b/, there a /b/, everywhere a /b/, /b/

Old MacDonald had a farm

Be-Bi-Be-Bi-Bo

And on this farm he had a _____ (Show or point out a new consonant; maybe *R.*)

Re-Ri-Re-Ri-Ro

With an /r/, /r/ here and an /r/, /r/ there
Here an /r/, there an /r/, everywhere an /r/, /r/,

Old MacDonald had a farm

Re-Ri-Re-Ri-Ro

And on this farm he had a _____ (Show or point out a new consonant.)

This can go on as long as children stay engaged. Be sure to only use consonants, as vowels will quickly cause you and the children to become frustrated! Once again, directing them to the print version while they are saying the sound is key to the intervention for students who are still weak in this skill. For some of those students, actually keeping up with the singing may be difficult. Rest assured that hearing the repeated sound as their classmates say it, seeing the letter as it is pointed out, and being submerged in the very rhythmic language can only improve phonemic awareness and phonics skills—in a painless way!

❖ Teach Phonemic awareness and phonics with "I've Been Working on the Railroad."

Teaching "I've Been Working on the Railroad" gives you a chance to integrate some history. This rich song represents an important era of America's growth. Pull out the United States map and give children background on how, why, and where the railroads were built. Then teach them this amusing and culturally rich song. Once they know it, use the last refrain only as a lively and effective intervention for students needing more letter/sound practice.

Early Reading Instruction & Intervention: A Sourcebook for PreK–2 © 2013 by Cindy Middendorf • Scholastic Teaching Resources

. . . and singing fee-fi-fiddly-i-o, fee-fi-fiddly-i-o

fee-fi-fiddly-i-o/Strumming on the old banjo

(Now, let's try t, /t/, t)

. . . and singing tee-ti-tiddly-i-o, tee-ti-tiddly-i-o

tee-ti-tiddly-i-o/Strumming on the old banjo

(Now, let's try s, /s/, s)

and singing see-si-siddly-i-o, see-si-siddly-i-o

see-si-siddly-i-o/Strumming on the old banjo

Again, you can continue, by using any consonants that you want to reinforce. Remember to show (or ask your Letter Finder to point out) each letter as you name it.

So many other songs! The phoneme-substitution strategy described above can be used with a lot of other popular songs. Think "Zip-a-Dee-Doo-Dah" (hippity-hoo-hah/hippity-hay) or substitute initial phonemes for "merrily" in "Row, Row, Row Your Boat" (berrily, berrily, berrily, berrily/life is but a bream) or, for first and second graders, use the nursery rhyme "Peter Piper" (Teter tiper ticked a teck of tickled teppers). Need more ideas? Just ask any "life-of-the-party" first- and second-grade students to play with language! Trust me, they won't disappoint you!

Fun Phonics Placemats

Materials: 12-inch-by-18-inch sheets of construction paper, markers

Invest some time (ask parent volunteers to help) in making fun, phonics-packed placemats to use during snack time or at a visually defined workspace (see page 63) for manipulatives. Simply use a 12-inch-by-18-inch piece of construction paper. Laminate the finished placemats, and you have transition tools that will have children practicing phonics and much more! They can "read" their placemat to a neighbor, or challenge each other to name all the given letters and sounds.

For younger learners, you could use colored dots or colored boxes for them to practice naming colors. Or use numbers and sets, number words, shapes, or simple math facts. Use these laminated mats to engage children in incidental reinforcement for anything that calls for practice: reading sight words, recognizing state abbreviations, reading fractions, or identifying road and safety signs. By using a heavy laminate, these learning mats can be wiped clean and will last through lot of snack times!

For a letters placemat, simply write 10–15 letters, uppercase beside lowercase, scattered over the placemat. Laminate the page, and you have a practice board that children can use to name letters as they are waiting for a snack or waiting for the manipulative they will be using for an activity you have planned. Encourage them to "read" their placemat to others at their table, naming the letters and giving the sound for each. For even more reinforcement, put a small picture beside each letter that begins with that letter's sound.

For a word family placemat, write a rime, preceded by a blank at the top of the paper; for example, _____ ot; _____ am; _____ ip. Randomly write as many consonants as you choose on the remainder of the paper. Challenge

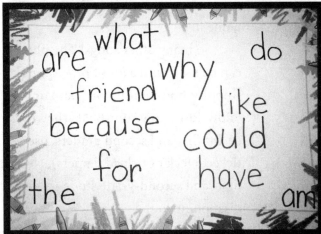

Placemats *During snack time or while waiting for manipulatives, keep students engaged with laminated placemats that reinforce instruction and encourage focused peer interaction.*

Early Reading Instruction & Intervention: A Sourcebook for PreK–2 © 2013 by Cindy Middendorf • Scholastic Teaching Resources

children to use waiting time to name the words they can create by blending the random consonants with the rime. You might choose to include consonants that would result in nonsense words, and ask children to determine if each word they create is real or nonsensical. Ask children to use the real words they create in a sentence.

Puzzle Pieces

Materials: jigsaw puzzle pieces, markers or crayons, basket

Admit it! Like most early childhood teachers, you have a 48-piece puzzle on your shelf that only has 43 pieces left! Yet you can't bear to throw it away because, well, you never know! Those missing pieces just might show up. (Never mind that they've been missing for three years!) As the ultimate "reduce, reuse, and recyclers," we early childhood educators can eventually find an instructional use for almost anything.

On a rainy afternoon, let children put together one or more of those puzzles. ("Oh, there are pieces missing? No kidding! What do you think that missing piece would look like?) Do not let students take the puzzle apart because once they are gone for the day, you will turn the puzzle into powerful intervention and learning center activities. Take four interconnecting pieces from a section of the puzzle. Take another four from a different section, and four more interconnecting pieces from another section. Lightly color the backs of each group with a different shade of the same color (or different designs of stripes, dots, stars, and so on). This color-coding will help your struggling learners decide which pieces belong together.

Using a permanent marker, write four words from one word family on the backs of one connected group of puzzle pieces (*hat, mat, bat, cat*); four words from another word family on the backs of the second section of puzzle pieces (*ham, bam, Sam, ram*); and four words from a third family on the backs of the third section of puzzle pieces (*tag, rag, sag, jag*). Break the sections apart, and put all 12 pieces in one basket.

> **TIP! COLOR HELPS THE VISUAL LEARNER**
>
> Instead of coloring the backs of each section of puzzle, you could simply use different colored markers to write on the backs. Children quickly learn that all letters (or numbers or shapes) written in red match others written in red, while all written in blue match others written in blue.

Puzzle Pieces *Putting together puzzle pieces requires kinesthetic, tactile, and visual modalities, while nurturing the visual-spatial intelligence. Use this strategy to reinforce a variety of skills.*

Children will assemble the word families as they fit the pieces together. Depending upon their skill level, you might choose to provide a recording sheet for them to list the words they assembled, add more words to each family, write one or more sentences using one or more words, or illustrate several of the words. As they work with partners, insist that children read each word.

Use the back of puzzle pieces to create engaging practice for matching uppercase and lowercase letters, for sequencing numbers, matching first and last names, or shapes with shape words. The time and effort you spend in creating the puzzle pieces will be rewarded year after year!

Puzzle Piece Recording Sheet *Children can record the words (number sequences, sentences) from their puzzle piece activity, and can add appropriate extensions.*

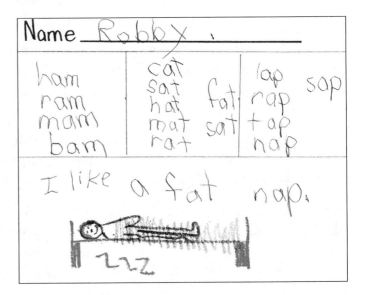

Tic-Tac-Go

Materials: paper and different colored markers, crayons, or pencils

Teach your children to play Tic-Tac-Toe with an academic twist that reinforces letters, sight words, shapes, or number recognition. Instead of using Xs and Os, one child is assigned (or chooses) a specific letter (uppercase and lowercase) and the other child is assigned (or chooses) a different letter. Or let each choose a different colored marker, crayon, or pencil, and write any letter (number, theme word, shape) they can think of as long as they can read the letter they wrote.

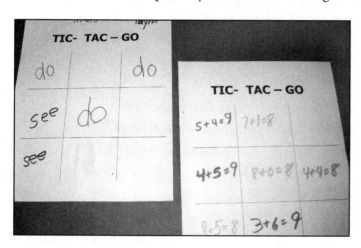

Children will be practicing skills while planning strategy (logical-mathematical and visual-spatial intelligences); working together (interpersonal intelligence); and using visual, auditory, and tactile modalities.

Tic Tac Go *Children practice visual planning, taking turns, and a variety of literacy and math skills with an ageless childhood favorite.*

Four Sides

Materials: Four Sides grid (see below); page protectors, fine-point dry-erase markers in different colors, old socks (optional)

Most of us played Four Sides as children. We started by making a grid of dots on a piece of paper, similar to this:

$$\begin{matrix} \cdot & \cdot & \cdot & \cdot & \cdot \\ \cdot & \cdot & \cdot & \cdot & \cdot \\ \cdot & \cdot & \cdot & \cdot & \cdot \\ \cdot & \cdot & \cdot & \cdot & \cdot \\ \cdot & \cdot & \cdot & \cdot & \cdot \end{matrix}$$

Partners would take turns connecting two dots either horizontally or vertically (never diagonally). The partner who put the fourth side on a box could claim the box by putting his or her initials in it. The player who "owned" the most boxes at the end of the game was declared the winner.

This strategy game can be used similarly to Tic-Tac-Go. As an intervention for struggling learners who need lots of reinforcement, assign each child a specific letter, number, sight word, math fact, shape, or vocabulary word to write in the box that he or she completes. As practice and reinforcement for more competent learners, allow each partner to use different colored pens, pencils, or markers, and write any sight word, number fact, or other target in his or her color. As with Tic-Tac-Go, players must read whatever they put in a box.

Prepare several templates for this game, keeping in mind that different skills will need boxes of different sizes. (Writing "2 + 3 = 5" will take more room than writing "Hh.") In addition, consider the fine motor skills of your learners when designing the size of the boxes.

Think and model environmentally green habits! Instead of having stacks of Four Sides sheets available, to be quickly used and discarded, allow partners to take one blank Four Sides sheet, slide it into a page protector, and use fine-point dry-erase markers of different colors to play. (See page 57.) Have old socks available for handy erasers and encourage multiple games with each partner choosing a new target word or number.

Baby Soda Bottles

Materials: baby soda bottles; letter or number beads; fine sand, salt, or sugar; colored sand

Most people teach because teaching is a passion, not a highly paid profession. Many teachers spend a lot of personal money on classroom materials. The materials that are worthy of our investment must be made to last and have multiple uses. Once I discovered the many ways in which I could use durable baby soda bottles, I eagerly invested!

Baby Soda Bottles *Baby soda bottles will engage reluctant learners in finding letters, making words, even graphing.*

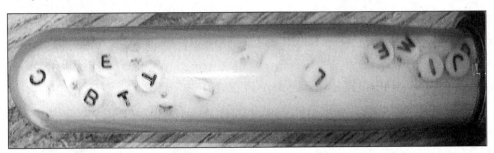

Early Reading Instruction & Intervention: A Sourcebook for PreK–2 © 2013 by Cindy Middendorf • Scholastic Teaching Resources

These clear, unbreakable test tubes with caps are actually two-liter soda bottles before they are blown and molded. They are available through most teacher-supply catalogs, and are marketed as the safest test tubes for science experiments at school. Sets of 6, 12, 18, or 30 are accompanied by a pamphlet of suggested uses.

Baby soda bottles can be used as intervention and support tools in several ways. Fill one about half full of fine sand, salt, or sugar. Add uppercase letter beads (available at craft stores and through several Web-based stores) and screw on the cap. Now children can shake and identify each letter they find, name its sound, write the letters and put the lowercase letter beside it, cross off each letter they find on an alphabet grid, or use the letters to make words.

Or buy number beads. Again, children can identify, write, and draw corresponding sets of number words, put the numbers in sequence, color them on a number grid, choose three that create a fact family, and so on. Use colored beads and ask children to create a simple graph to show which colors appeared after each shake.

For younger students, fill each bottle with a different level of colored sand and allow them to arrange the tubes in order from greatest amount of sand to least amount of sand. Since the caps are flat, these nifty tubes will stand straight up.

TIP!

Don't spend a king's ransom on colored sand. Simply use inexpensive playground sand. Mix it with enough dry tempera paint in a zippered plastic bag to achieve the desired color.

KaBoom!

Materials: index cards, marker

We all know the child who raises his or her hand even before you ask the question. When you actually ask for an answer, this very active learner, arm waving in the air, often responds, "Um, um . . . I forgot." Strongly kinesthetic learners, as well as many learners with hyperactive tendencies, raise their hands simply because you asked a question, which implies permission to move!

Engage those movers and shakers while practicing skills. Play KaBoom! in small or whole groups, when waiting in line for the rest of the class to join, or on the rug with the first 10 or 12 who arrive and are ready. It is simple, fast, and can last 30 seconds or 10 minutes. KaBoom! provides practice, support, reinforcement, and that all-important component of learning: movement.

The level of your children and the targeted skill will dictate how you prepare your KaBoom! cards. Write one letter (or vocabulary word, phrase, shape, number, sight word, number fact, or child's name) on an index card. Write KaBoom! on several other cards, and intersperse these KaBoom! cards randomly among the others. Children must read (recite, name) the letter (word, phrase, shape, or number) on each card, but when they see a KaBoom! card, they must put both arms straight into the air and say, "KaBoom!"

All children will be intently looking at the cards, anticipating the KaBoom! Each struggling learner will be hearing the other students name the letter, word, phrase, shape, or number they see. All will benefit from the movement—and the oxygen infusion to the brain—that results from the vigorous lifting of their arms. If shouts of "KaBoom!" are more than you can bear, make it a silent "KaBoom!" Instead of saying the word, students lift their arms powerfully into the air when a KaBoom! card appears.

To extend the activity, remove each KaBoom! card after it appears, but keep cycling through the rest of the cards. Children soon realize, "Hey, we went through that whole pile twice! You were taking out the KaBooms!"

Water Paint the Walls

Materials: one or more plastic gallon jugs filled with water; plastic tubs or dishpans, small plastic cups or containers; large paintbrushes or toy brooms; small dry-erase board

Water painting, whether on walls or pavement, is an engaging, outside activity with powerful inherent benefits. If possible, use the outside walls of the school building, since a vertical surface forces more vigorous large muscle movement, stretching, and core involvement. However, water painting with children's toy brooms on the pavement can be effective as well.

On a mild day, assign a child to fill one or more plastic gallon jugs with water. Ask other children to carry the jugs outside. Have other children take out one or more tubs or dishpans to pour the water into, small plastic cups or containers that each child will use to scoop water from the tub, and let others carry out large

Early Reading Instruction & Intervention: A Sourcebook for PreK–2 © 2013 by Cindy Middendorf • Scholastic Teaching Resources

paintbrushes (or brooms). Once outside, appoint one or more children to pour the water into the tubs. Keep the tubs far enough away from one another to avoid traffic jams as children dip their individual cups into the water. Assign each child an area of the wall or pavement on which to paint. As you call out a letter, word, or number fact, each child uses the paintbrush (or broom) to write the word in water. By writing the correct response on a small, hand-held dry-erase board, you can provide immediate feedback. Ask students to write the next word directly under the first. On warm, sunny days, the first word will have evaporated before the second word is finished. If work space is limited, allow children to work in groups of two or three, each taking a turn on the wall while the others provide help as needed.

Once children have done outside water painting several times, allow them to take the materials out during recess time and paint whatever they wish on the walls. They will use lots of large muscle groups and become very creative. I once had a little fellow with Asperger's syndrome who had previously encountered all sorts of difficult challenges on the playground, both socially and physically. When this student discovered wall painting with water, he would beg to paint bricks during recess. Very methodically, he would cover as many bricks as he could with water. As they evaporated, he would repaint. He began reaching higher and higher and stretching his arms farther and farther. It was calming to him, and it provided a focus he had been missing before. That calm and repetitive recess activity made for more peaceful afternoons. Not a miracle cure, surely, but a self-soothing activity that worked for this student.

Towers

Materials: Jenga game, a large piece of felt, fine-point permanent marker, basket

Access all modalities and nurture visual/spatial intelligence while reinforcing skills by teaching children to play Towers. Shop yard sales, secondhand stores, or inquire among friends, families of your class, or colleagues to find an old Jenga game. Jenga is played with 54 wooden blocks. (*Note:* You don't need to use all 54 blocks.)

Blocks are of different lengths, but all stack neatly to create a tower. The tower is built by arranging an initial base of blocks that is three inches square. Subsequent levels are built by crisscrossing the pattern of blocks. Once all blocks have been used to create a tower, players take turns carefully removing one block at a time until eventually the tower tumbles.

Decide how to best use your tower blocks. Will you use them to support and practice letter recognition? Sight words? Shapes? Numbers? Number words? Colors? Write one target word (letter, shape, and so on,) on each block using a fine-point permanent marker. Put all the blocks in a basket, and invite three to four players to play. The first player draws a block, reads the letter and gives its sound (or reads the word), and lays the block in the middle of the table. Play continues until all blocks have been used. Now the play reverses, as players must remove one block at a time without toppling the tower. Of course, when a child pulls out a block, he or she must read it. In the younger grades, Towers is best played without keeping score. Simply ask all players to help one another read the blocks. To make the game more competitive for older learners, allow a point for each block read correctly, both when building the tower and when removing blocks. Subtract five points from the score of the player who initiates the ultimate toppling!

> ### TONE DOWN THE TOWER TUMBLING!
>
> Spread a large piece of felt across the table where the tower will be built. When the blocks come tumbling down, the felt will buffer some of the noise!

Stretch-and-Say Bands for Decoding and Blending

Materials: elastic (1½ to 2 inches wide), scissors, permanent marker, duct tape

Learning to decode (sound out) and learning to blend phonemes into a word doesn't just happen (Carnine, et al., 2004). It takes conscious practice and focused instruction. Flash cards, word wheels, and word pulls all provide repetition and rehearsal. The more we vary the modes of practice, the better children become at decoding and blending. Stretch-and-Say bands engage multiple modalities and provide a welcome change from flash cards.

Buy wide elastic from any sewing notions or arts and crafts store. Cut it into 3-inch lengths. Use a permanent marker to write a different consonant-vowel-

Early Reading Instruction & Intervention: A Sourcebook for PreK–2 © 2013 by Cindy Middendorf • Scholastic Teaching Resources

consonant word on each band; for example, I would write all the short-*a* words in red, all short- *i* words in green, all short-*o* words in blue, and so on. As you stretch out the sounds orally, slowly stretch the band. Children delight in matching their voice to the stretch they see. Once the letters have been stretched and sounded out, snap the band back together to blend the sounds into one word.

Once you model this activity for the whole group, allow children to work with partners to decode and blend words. The bands can be put in a center where children say the word, and perhaps make a list of the words they successfully decoded and blended, and choose three or more to use in sentences.

A word of warning: The bands get used—a lot! The ends of the elastic may begin to fray. To avoid the unraveling, you can affix duct tape over each end or sew a seam down each end of the band.

Stretch and Say *What a fun way to practice decoding and blending! Children see the letters stretch as they say each sound. When they blend, the elastic band snaps to see the word.*

Arm Spelling

Materials: alphabet chart, pointer (optional)

Work out the wiggles, engage the kinesthetic modality, and reinforce letter recognition, sight words, or spelling words with Arm Spelling. Direct children's attention to an alphabet chart that shows uppercase and lowercase letters. If the alphabet chart does not show the handwriting lines (the baseline, the midline, the top line), demonstrate how the uppercase and lowercase letters would look on each: *"Every letter sits between the baseline and the midline. Some also go above the midline to the top line, and others go below the baseline.*

"Let's pretend that our waistline is the baseline on our paper. Our shoulders will be the midline, and above our head is the top line. We'll use our arm to show the size of some of the lowercase letters. Look at the lowercase a *on the alphabet chart. We'd show it with our arm like this."* (Bend your arm so that your elbow rests near your waist and your fist is level with your shoulder.) *"Let's show a lowercase* b." (Extend your arm straight up into the air.) *"How would a lowercase* g *look?"* (Elbow at

waist, fist straight down beside the outside thigh.)

"*Now let's say each letter of the alphabet and move our arm to show its size and position.*" A student with a long pointer can walk along the alphabet chart, pointing out each letter as it is demonstrated. Seeing the visual representation of the letter, along with the auditory (children hear the letter name) and the kinesthetic (children move their arm to show the letter's size), provides multiple neurological pathways for imbedding learning.

Once children are comfortable with the activity, extend their thinking: "*Let's all arm spell our own first name. Ready, go!*" Allow several seconds for children to simultaneously arm spell their names, and then ask, "*Why did all of you begin with your arm extended into the air?*" (because each name starts with a capital letter). Encourage children to find a classmate whose name would be arm spelled identically to his or her own (i.e., Ian and Sam would use the same arm movements, as would Cindy and Marty).

Ask children who are competent with letter recognition to "arm the alphabet," but to say the sound for each letter instead of its name. Once again, ask one child to point to each letter as its sound is named. Whenever we connect the visual to the auditory, we are giving additional support to our at-risk learners while reinforcing learning for all children.

Have students practice sight words by arm spelling the letters as they spell the word. More competent students can challenge one another to guess the sight word represented by the arm movements. First- and second-grade students could be encouraged to practice spelling words by arm spelling them with a partner. Challenge them to find words from the spelling (or sight word) list that would have the same arm movements, such as *clean* and *stare* or *it* and *of.* One partner could arm spell from a list of spelling words, and the other partner could decide which word is being spelled.

Configured Spelling

Materials: graph paper, crayon or marker, scissors, poster paper

Configured Spelling has the same premise as Arm Spelling. Once children can visualize the tall letters, short letters, and below-the-line letters, handwriting loses

Early Reading Instruction & Intervention: A Sourcebook for PreK–2 © 2013 by Cindy Middendorf • Scholastic Teaching Resources

some of its mystery. Strong visual learners appreciate the connection, and all other learners need the connection!

Provide graph paper with grids of an appropriate size for your children. (See page 62.) Choose an appropriate word to model. A first-grade teacher may choose a word such as *apple*. With children, count the number of letters. Draw a baseline that includes five vertical boxes, one for each letter. In the first box, write the letter *a*. In the next box, write the letter *p*, with the circle of the *p* inside the box, and the tail extending below the drawn baseline, into the box below. Continue writing the word, pointing out the placement of each letter. When finished, use a crayon or marker to trace around the word, making the configuration very obvious.

Early in the year, have children configure their own names. Let them cut out and compare the shape of their own name with one another to see if there are matching configurations among classmates' names.

Ask children to write and trace the configurations of several sight words to add a visual/spatial dimension to sight word practice. Abler students could configure words, cut them out and trace them on poster paper. You can also cut out the blank configuration to provide templates for students to match words to shapes. Students struggling with sight words should match configurations or actually configure the same three or four words daily for several days.

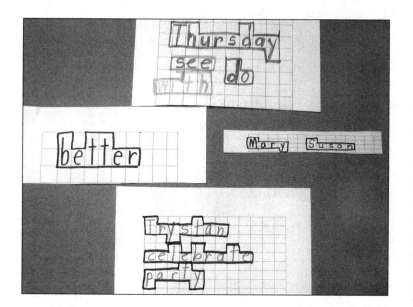

Encourage children to use Configured Spelling to practice spelling lists. Working individually or in pairs, they can create their own templates to practice (or challenge)!

Configured Spelling *Nurture visual-spatial intelligence and engage the visual modality with configured spelling on graph paper.*

Word Ladders

Materials: paper, marker

How often have your young readers read *sit* for *sat* or *bat* for *bad* or randomly replaced a phoneme? No matter how often we say, "Good readers look at the whole word," many children still glance at and call words. And if they develop that careless habit with consonant-vowel-consonant words, imagine how it impacts their reading of words with two or more syllables. Struggling readers, especially, often look at the first one or two letters of a word and take a guess. But through practice, they can learn that changing one simple letter can change a word completely, and they prove that they've acquired this knowledge when they create Word Ladders.

Get all your readers to pay attention to the difference one letter can make in a word's pronunciation and meaning. Start with a consonant-vowel-consonant word on the bottom rung of a hand-drawn ladder. Challenge children to change only one letter at a time to make a new word. Continue up the ladder, changing only one letter at a time. Insist that each rung have a real word, not a nonsense word.

Ask struggling learners to make ladders of word families by changing only the first letter on each rung. Challenge more confident students to change any letter, one at a time, as they move up the ladder. I once allowed kindergarten students to draw their own ladders, and to continue changing one letter at a time until they could go no further. Two little girls worked off and on for days, taping sheet after sheet of paper together until they had six sheets, each with ladders of seven or eight rungs, each rung showing a new word. Their first ladder started with the word *ham*. At the top of their last ladder was the word *jet*. They were proud to inform me that they "could have gone to the sky with our ladder."

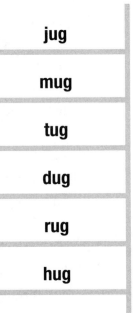

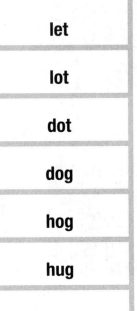

Syllable Match

Materials: index cards, poster board, or construction paper in different colors; markers

Just as some kindergarten and first-grade children will look at the first consonant and vowel in a word and guess without noting the ending consonant, so too will many first and second graders read one syllable of a word and guess the rest. Many below-grade readers need practice in seeing syllables and chunks within words. Like Word Ladders, Syllable Match reinforces the importance of looking at the whole word as children match up first and second syllables to make real (not nonsense!) words.

To prepare Syllable Match cards, write the first syllables of each of the words in the box below on one color of index cards, poster board, or construction paper. Write all the second syllables on a different color. For instance, all first syllables might be on blue, while all second syllables might be on yellow.

Play is similar to any memory match game. Players begin by working together to assemble 10, 15, or 20 words or whatever number you assign. If they have 10 words, they would have 20 cards; 15 words will use 30 cards (one card for each syllable). Cards are thoroughly mixed and laid facedown. Players take turns turning over a blue card (first syllable) and then a yellow card (second syllable). If the two cards can make a real word, the player keeps the cards.

Syllable Match does more than just give practice in noticing syllables. It also provides intervention for children who need practice in decoding consonant-vowel-consonant words. To use as a vocabulary intervention activity, ask players to list each word they collected and to either write it in a sentence, find and write a definition for it, or list two or three synonyms.

Suggested Words for Syllable Match				
nap kin	spi der	pic nic	kit ten	ten nis
hun dred	mag net	trum pet	num ber	mar ket
rob ber	tab let	den tist	pep per	win ner
hel met	wit ness	vic tim	com bat	cob web
hap pen	plas tic	nos tril	fin ish	les son
muf fin	doc tor	pen guin	free dom	sun set

Real and Nonsense Draw

Materials: two small containers, such as a half-pint milk carton; colorful adhesive-backed paper, index cards of different colors, marker

This simple activity not only guides children in decoding and blending practice, but also in discerning real from nonsense words. Being able to decode consonant-short vowel-consonant words marks one of the earliest reading successes children achieve. They quickly learn that not all words that can be "read" are real words.

TIP!

Make the consonant cards one color (most logically, the same color as the "Consonants" box or basket) and the word family ending cards another color. The visual clue will help at cleanup time.

You'll need two small containers, each a different color. (I like to use the bottom of half-pint milk cartons covered with colorful, adhesive-backed paper.) Label one container "Consonants" and the other "Word Family Endings" (also known by the literacy term *rime*, which refers to a syllable beginning with a vowel that is followed by one or more consonants. You might choose to label the second box "Rimes.") Prepare consonant cards by writing one consonant on each of several cards. Use as many or as few consonants as you find appropriate for your class. On the other cards, write several word family endings (e.g., *-ot*, *-ap*, *-im*, *-et*, *-ug*).

Real/Nonsense Bags and Real/Nonsense Recording Sheet *Children draw a consonant (or blend) and line it up with a word ending. After reading the word, they decide if it is a real or a nonsense word. In addition to simply recording the words and noting "real" or "nonsense" (happy or surprised face), children can use the words they created in sentences.*

Without looking, children draw one card from each container and put the consonant in front of the word family ending to create a consonant-vowel-consonant word. Each child reads the word. If the word is real, he or she could be asked to use it in a sentence. If it is not a real word, the child declares, "Nonsense!"

As a center activity, children record each word they create. By drawing a happy face or a surprised face beside each, they can indicate whether the word is real (happy face) or nonsensical (surprised face).

Letter/Word Hopscotch

Materials: hopscotch mat: window shade, sturdy plastic tablecloth, or shower curtain; permanent marker or masking tape; set of laminated cards (alphabet, sight words, number facts, shapes, colors, and so on); double-sided tape or poster putty

Hopscotch in PreK and kindergarten has its own rules (or lack of rules!) and is a powerful means of strengthening the core, exercising large muscles, and developing coordination. For many children, the irresistible urge to jump makes hopscotch a perfect phonics intervention. Create a blank hopscotch board on an old window shade, sturdy plastic tablecloth, or shower curtain. Prepare and laminate a set of alphabet cards (or sight words, number facts, shapes, colors, and so on). Place a small strip of double-sided tape (or a piece of poster putty) on the back of enough cards so that you can put a card in the upper left corner of each hopscotch box or in the middle of double boxes. Now as the child hops, he or she names each letter and gives its sound (reads the sight word or identifies the number or shape). Let a group of "cheerleaders" stand around the hopscotch mat to encourage and offer help as necessary.

Because the double-sided tape (or poster putty) allows easy placement and removal of the laminated cards, they can be quickly changed. Once you've modeled how to play and practiced with the entire class, take the hopscotch mat to the playground. Make more than one mat so several groups can hop at once. Keep the laminated cards and the tape or poster putty in a lunchbox or another easily transportable carrier.

The hopscotch mats can also help turn indoor recess into active learning time. Push aside tables and chairs, lay out several mats, and let children divide into groups and choose which cards to use. A welcome energy release on a gloomy day!

Letter/Word Twister

Materials: *Twister mat (window shade, sturdy plastic tablecloth, or shower curtain; permanent markers: red, yellow, green, blue); index cards of different colors; double-sided tape; box or other container*

Just as we use old window shades, plastic tablecloths, or shower curtains to create hopscotch boards, we can also use them to make fun Twister games. A Twister mat is simply a plastic mat with four rows of large colored circles, each row with four different colors: red, yellow, green, blue. For classroom use, it is not necessary to have circles of different colors, but it certainly adds more variations to the game.

Instead of using the traditional spinner, I made and laminated two stacks of colored cards. Each card in the blue stack said "left foot," "right foot," "left hand," or "right hand." The second stack of cards can vary depending upon which skill you want to support. I wrote letters on yellow cards, sight words on white cards, children's names on green cards, shapes on pink cards, and numbers with number words on orange cards. When we were ready to play, I would choose a stack of content cards, slap double-sided tape on the back, and stick them to the Twister mat, each just outside of, but touching a circle. (If you fasten a card within a circle, little hands and feet will quickly mangle it!)

Choose two people to be the callers. One will have the stack of hands-and-feet cards; the other will name a content card on the mat beside an empty circle. Two other children will be the players, who take turns maneuvering around each other to put, for example, a left hand on the word *would* or a right foot on the letter *B/b*. As soon as one player slips or moves a hand or foot out of an assigned circle, he or she is replaced by another player. Keep rotating players and callers. I found it worked well to have about eight children around the mat at any time. Play goes fairly quickly, and no one stands around for too long without being involved.

Just like Letter/Word Hopscotch, Twister works best if you have two or three mats being used simultaneously. This, too, makes a great recess game to take outside. Keep the mats, laminated cards, and double-sided tape in a convenient box or carrier for simple transport. Like color highlighting tape (page 58), double-sided tape can be reused if the pieces are returned to a large laminated card and covered with another card. You can also teach children to loop a small piece of

Early Reading Instruction & Intervention: A Sourcebook for PreK–2 © 2013 by Cindy Middendorf • Scholastic Teaching Resources

masking tape into piece of double-sided tape.

Add Twister to your recess backup plan when children must stay inside. Again, push aside chairs and tables. Be prepared for lots of laughing, and remember, laughing is good for learning!

Musical Letter/Word Chairs

Materials: laminated content cards, recorded music

Musical Chairs, like Letter/Word Hopscotch and Twister, keeps children busy and focused during indoor recess or on a gloomy Friday afternoon. Use the laminated content cards (letters, weight words, spelling words, shapes, numbers) that you've prepared for Letter/Word Hopscotch or Twister. Arrange chairs in a circle, making certain there is one chair for each player.

> TIP!
>
> Arrange two or three circles of chairs. Twenty-five children? Make two circles of eight and one of nine, or one group of 12 and another of 13.

Place one letter card (or spelling word card, sight word card, vocabulary card, number or number fact card) face down on each chair. Turn on the music. Just as in the traditional game of musical chairs, children march around in a circle until the music stops. Each child picks up a card from the chair in front of him or her, sits in that chair, and reads the card to the group. Unlike the traditional game, *no chair is removed*. Every child plays every time. Children stand, place the card facedown on the chair, and listen for the music to begin again.

Fly Away

Materials: *laminated content cards; round tablecloth, flat bed sheet, or parachute; whistle or bell (optional)*

Fly Away can be an indoor recess game or an energizing pick-me-up on a rainy afternoon. Once again, use the laminated cards you've prepared for letters, sight words, class names, spelling words, shapes, numbers, or number facts.

Use a round tablecloth, a flat bed sheet, or a real parachute, if one is available.

With the tablecloth, sheet, or parachute on the floor (or outside on the ground), spread the cards out in the middle. Ask children to stand around the outside of the tablecloth and grab the edges. They begin slowly lifting and lowering the cloth "parachute" so it gently ripples. Initially, their job is to keep the cards on the parachute while the cards drift slowly up and down. At your cue, the children begin to chant:

"Little cards, little cards, floating around,

How many cards can we get on the ground?"

Students begin to count to 10, or by tens to 100, or by twos to 20, or by fives to 50 (or ask them to recite the ABCs). While counting or reciting, they begin to vigorously shake the parachute, attempting to throw the cards off. At your cue (a word, a whistle, a bell), children lay the parachute flat, find a card that flew off of it, and return to their original spot with the card. Each child shows and reads his or her card. Then they toss all the cards back into the middle; children march counterclockwise while counting or they stop and play again.

If you are using smaller round tablecloths, have two games going. The smaller the parachute, the easier it is to make the cards fly off.

Say It, Say It, Rhyme It

The ability to identify and create rhyming words is a fundamental phonological awareness skill. Children who cannot hear and create rhymes will have difficulty in learning to decode and blend words (Goswami, 1999), since a child who cannot hear patterns in words will struggle to see patterns in words. Rhyming is crucial! A simple twist turns a recess favorite into fun rhyming practice for all and important intervention for those still struggling with rhyming.

Practice rhyming with an active, engaging game of Say It, Say It, Rhyme It using the traditional Duck, Duck, Goose format. Whisper a word for which there are multiple rhyming words to the child who is "It." To introduce the activity, and for younger children, simple one-syllable, vowel-consonant-vowel words work best (e.g., *hat, mop, pet*). The child who is "It" walks behind a circle of seated children, touching each head while saying the target word: "mop, mop, mop, mop." Before completing the circle, "It" must touch a head and say a rhyming word, "top!" The child whose head is touched when the rhyming word is given

Early Reading Instruction & Intervention: A Sourcebook for PreK–2 © 2013 by Cindy Middendorf • Scholastic Teaching Resources

stands and chases "It" around the outside of the circle. "It" is safe when he or she reaches and sits in the spot left open by the chaser. The chaser now becomes "It."

The game can also be played by having "It" continue to name rhyming words; the chaser will be the child who is touched when "It" says a word that does not rhyme; for example, Denny might touch heads as he says, "mouse, house, louse, touse, rabbit," and, of course, the child who is touched on "rabbit" becomes the chaser. Allowing children to use nonsense rhyming words is, of course, easier, while asking for only real words will make the activity more challenging. Consider the skill level of the group (or of "It") when designing the rules.

Adapt and adjust the format based on the level and needs of your students. Encourage older children to think of their own target word. Younger children, or those struggling with rhyming, may need you to whisper both a target word and a rhyming word. With an especially large class, divide children into two or three circles to allow more to have a turn. Say It, Say It, Rhyme It can be played outside or as an indoor recess game.

Letter/Word Blizzard Balls

Materials: recycled paper, pencils

Let children use paper from the recycling box for this activity. Direct each child to write a word, letter, spelling word, first name, shape, number, or number fact on a scrap of paper. Model how to write or draw in large letters with a firm hand so that the word or shape can be easily seen from a distance. As an intervention for struggling learners, assign specific words to specific children. As reinforcement and practice, allow children to choose what they will write or draw on their paper.

Now for the fun part! Tell children to wad their paper up into a paper snowball. Place half of the class on one side of the room, the rest on the other side, facing the other team. At your cue, they must throw their "snowballs" into the center of the room. At your next cue, they go into the center, grab a snowball, and return to their side of the room. Each child unwinds the snowball, shows it to the rest of the class, and reads it (or, for spelling words, reads and spells it).

The snowballs can be wadded again, tossed, retrieved, and read. For a more competitive activity, award each team a point for each snowball it correctly reads or identifies.

CHAPTER 5

Sight Words

A solid command of sight word vocabulary and instant identification of those high-frequency words gives beginning readers a leg up. Literacy experts tell us that 50–75 percent of all text consists of sight words. Not only does sight word mastery impact fluency, and therefore, comprehension, but it also gives young readers a sense of success.

Sight Word Mastery: What Do Tier I Teachers Need to Know?

Practice makes permanent! Sight words, many of which cannot be phonetically decoded, must be reviewed, used, played with, pointed out, and incorporated until the words are so familiar that students can read them with automaticity. Flash cards are, at best, a monotonous way to drill, and they can turn literacy practice into a grueling, hopeless, and frustrating exercise for struggling students. Differentiation, brain-friendly instruction, research-based best practice, and common sense dictate that we intervene with engaging, active, playful approaches for building this important skill.

> "The business of teaching beginning reading is to . . . get the mechanics of reading rapidly and thoroughly in hand so that the child may quickly arrive at the thought-getting, thought-expressing period. To do this, the teacher, regardless of what method or mixture of methods she affects, must teach sight words until the pupils know readily all the good everyday helping words which they will need all their lives in reading. For if a child has to hesitate over these in the next grade, how is he ever to find time to puzzle out all the hard new words?"
>
> —from *Practical Methods, Aids and Devices for Teachers* by Walter J. Beecher & Grace B. Faxon, Volume 1, 1916

Research specifically involving at-risk students has shown that those children in particular learn sight words more readily and with better results when the instruction includes interactive games (Meadan, Stoner, & Parette, 2008). All children master sight word vocabulary through their own unique learning blueprint, just as they learn all other early literacy skills. It follows, then, that we early childhood teachers need to provide a wide range of visual, auditory, kinesthetic, and tactile experiences to support mastery of sight words.

Tier 1 Quality Instruction and Interventions for Sight Word Vocabulary

Perhaps you remember learning sight words the way I do: endless stacks of flashcards. A very well-meaning adult would stack the cards into two piles as I bumbled my way through: one stack held the words I could name, and the other stack held the ones I couldn't name. Never have I encountered a child who, upon seeing a teacher approach with flashcards, responded, "Hooray! I get to do flashcards!" The following activities are both kid- and teacher-friendly. These strategies engage children and give them repeated exposure to and practice with sight words.

The Crowned Heads of Sight Words

Materials: a blank, colored crown for each student, marker

Make sight word practice a royal experience! Create sight word crowns that you can use year after year. Recycle your old bulletin board borders by cutting them into strips that can be stapled into a crown. You might also check teacher-supply stores and catalogs for colored crowns that are blank or collect the crowns given with children's meals at some fast-food restaurants and turn them inside out.

On each crown, write a different sight word. On a specified day (or portion of a day), crown each child the prince or princess of "do," "what," or "off" or any other sight word. Children address each other as "Prince Could" or "Princess Was" and practice reading one another's words.

Take five minutes on your Royal Sight Word Day to play Inside-Outside. Divide the class into two groups. One group forms a circle in which everyone faces outward. The other group forms a circle around the first group, with everyone facing a prince or princess from the inside group. (If the circles have an uneven number of students, wear a crown yourself or ask a child to stop and start the music) As music plays, one circle slides in a clockwise direction to the rhythm; the other circle slides in a counterclockwise direction. When the music stops, the prince or princess in the inside circle bows or curtsies to the prince(s) or princess(es) in the outside circle and reads the sight word on the crown and says,

"Good morning, Prince Saw," or "Good morning, Princess You," depending, of course, on the sight word crown the royal is wearing. The prince or princess in the outside circle returns the curtsy, and the music begins again.

When you initially pass out the crowns, ask children to write their royal word in their own word journal. This gives them an opportunity to practice the word and to have help reading it if necessary. I was pleased to find that even though children could not see their own crown, they became very possessive of their word for the day. Whenever crowns were passed out, I would hear children call, "Hey, Elena has my word from last time! I was 'Princess See' last time!"

If you prefer, choose only one student to be a prince and one to be a princess on any given day. Let them wear the crown for the entire day and encourage classmates to address them by their royal name for the day. This adaptation is a good way to introduce and reinforce new sight words that you are adding to the word wall.

Sight Word Necklaces

Materials: index cards, hole-puncher, long shoelace or heavy-duty twine, plastic pockets (optional)

Like a Sight Word Crown, a Sight Word Necklace lets children connect with and take ownership of a sight word. Each child wears a sight word necklace for the day and uses every opportunity to ask classmates to read the word. Hand out the necklaces randomly or assign specific words to specific children based on what you know about their need to practice a particular word.

The necklaces can be made using index cards. After laminating each card, use a hole-puncher to make two holes and then string a loop of long shoelace or heavy-duty twine through the holes. Or you can purchase miniature plastic pockets from a discount or office supply store. They are inexpensive, sturdy, easy to slide word cards in and out of, and last indefinitely. Like the crowns in the previous activity, once you make a set of necklaces, you can use them year after year.

VISUALS ADD A NEURAL CONNECTION

When teaching sight words, use any eccentric trick that works! I was delighted to find a Web site that allowed me to download and print free visuals for many of the sight words (www.spookysmouse.com/kidcrowns/kidscrowns.html). The creative designers of this site suggest that we introduce a word with a memory trick to fortify learning; for example, the word *of* is written beside a picture of a dove ("the dove of *of*"); the word *saw* is written on the picture of a paw ("the paw of *saw*"), and the word *are* is printed by a star ("the star of *are*"). For some children, these silly but effective rhymes may be the glue that makes sight words stick!

Sight Word Sticks

Materials: craft sticks, marker, container

Write each sight word on a craft stick. Keep the sticks in a container, and as children line up to leave for lunch, a special class, or dismissal, have them walk by the container and pull out a stick. Just before you leave the room, after everyone is lined up, each child must read his or her stick to you and then return it to the container. Because students draw a stick on their way to lining up, they have time to get help reading the word from a friend if necessary.

Door Words

Materials: index cards and marker (or a set of sight word cards), tape

As you teach a new sight word, write it on an index card and attach it to the wall or doorframe outside your room. When children return to the classroom from lunch or a special class, each of them should point to one of the words and read it as his or her "entrance exam" into the room. Since I could not always be standing at the door as children filed in, I taught them to pay close attention to everyone in front of them to make sure that each word was read correctly and to offer help when needed.

Highlighter Hunt

Materials: a variety of pieces of text (junk mail, magazine pages, newspaper sections, old greeting cards, travel brochures), baskets (optional), highlighters, magnifying glasses or children's sunglasses

Children love highlighters! And they don't need to able to read an entire text in order to find the sight words in a given piece of text. Save junk mail. Rip pages from magazines. Cut up newspapers into sections. Gather old greeting cards. Bring in tourist pamphlets from hotel racks. Almost anything that has a fair amount of print on it will have dozens of sight words.

Stack the text pieces in several piles or put them in baskets. At a center, ask children to track the print, line by line, and highlight each sight word they find.

Magnifying glasses or children's sunglasses with the lenses removed help keep children engaged. Once they highlight the words, children read them to a partner or write a list of them. I have found that, without prompting, many children tally the number of times they found specific words repeated in the text.

Encourage children to take their highlighted text home and read the sight words to their families.

Grrrr . . .! Sticks

Materials: craft sticks, markers, can

Write sight words at the end of individual craft sticks. As an intervention for struggling students, choose three to five sight words that cause problems for these learners. Write a word on several different sticks so that players have repeated practice with specifically targeted words. As support and reinforcement for all students, write a different sight word on each of 20 or 25 sticks. For every five or six sticks that you mark with a sight word, write "Grrrr . . .!" on another stick and draw a grouchy face. Put all the sticks, word end down, in a can.

Two or more children take turns pulling a stick. If they can read the word, they keep the stick and pass the can to the next player. If they need help reading the word, the stick goes back into the can. When a "Grrr . . .!" stick is drawn, the child makes a scrunched-up face, clenches his or her fists, and say in a most annoyed voice, "Grrr . . .!" That child then puts all the sticks he or she has accumulated back into the can.

This game can last for as many minutes as you determine. If you allow it, children will go around the circle endlessly, reading words, dramatically growling, and collecting and returning sight word sticks. You can make this activity more finite by setting a limit on the number of turns each child has: "After each of you has had six turns, count your sticks and declare a winner!"

Magnetics

Materials: small magnetic board, set of magnetic letters and numbers

Most of us have a large-group meeting area in our room. We gather the class there, often on a carpet, to do read-alouds, shared readings, class meetings, and other activities that involve the entire class. Typically, we sit in a chair facing the class. Prepare that area with plenty of "at-your-fingertip" tools to make the most of every second spent there. One essential is a small magnetic board and a set of magnetic letters (and numbers).

As children are coming up and settling on the carpet for whole-group time, turn those waiting minutes into instructional minutes. Pull out the magnetic board, along with several letters that will spell a sight word and engage children in figuring out which sight word you have in mind.

Suppose you want to quickly review the word *what*. Put the *w* on the board and ask children to guess which sight word you have in mind. (It is important to have children facing your word wall or to have a large, laminated list of sight words displayed in the whole-group meeting area.) Next add an *h* beside the *w*. Let any child who is seated on the rug take part in the guessing. Once someone names the word, ask everyone to name the remaining letters. Take another second to clap out the spelling or to arm spell the word (see page 83). Bingo! The whole process takes less than 30 seconds, and it injects valuable reinforcement into time that is often wasted as you wait for everyone to settle on the rug.

For a more challenging activity, put all the letters for one sight word in random order on the board. To reinforce the word *what*, you might arrange the magnetic letters to spell *hwta*. Challenge children to brainstorm with one or more partners to fix the sight word. Once the code has been cracked, ask them to chorally spell the word. Correct their spelling as necessary. Once again, arm spell the word for a kinesthetic connection or ask students to use the sight word in a sentence.

Overhead Sight Words

Materials: *overhead projector; sight word cards; basket; magnetic, foam, or cut-out letters; blank pieces of paper; tape*

Chances are good that in a dusty back corner of a storeroom somewhere in your building lurks an old overhead projector. Track it down, rescue it from oblivion, dust it off, plug it in, and turn it on for novel sight word work. You don't need lots of space for an overhead projector center. You simply need floor space not far from an outlet where the projector can shine onto a blank wall.

Put a basket of sight word cards at the center, along with a couple of sets of magnetic letters. Have children come to the center in groups of two or more. They take turns drawing a sight word card, using the letters to spell it out on the overhead, and asking their partners to read the word on the wall. (Children nurture and strengthen visual-spatial intelligence as they figure out which way to lay letters so that they project correctly onto the wall.)

Extend the learning by allowing children to tape a blank piece of paper to the wall. Once a word is written on the overhead projector, a child can trace it on the paper from its projection on the wall. With careful placing of letters, children can fit many words on one piece of paper (depending, of course, on the size of the paper and the size of the letters being used).

The Sight Word Ball

Materials: several rubber or plastic beach balls, permanent marker

This drill was one of my favorites as a little girl. I had a wonderful fourth-grade teacher who let us practice multiplication facts by using a beach ball. It was a novel idea back then, but now many teachers use balls to practice all kinds of rote skills.

Buy several rubber or plastic beach balls. Using a permanent marker, write sight words randomly all over the balls. Put a dot or draw a line under each word so that their right-side-up position is obvious. (The last thing struggling learners need is to attempt to read an upside down word!)

Ask children to sit on the floor in a circle, legs apart, forming a V. The first child rolls the ball into the V of another's legs. That child grabs the ball and reads the sight word that lies closest to his or her right thumb. The players on either side of the reader confirm that the word has been read correctly. They are also responsible for helping when necessary.

To allow more children to have more turns, divide your class into two or three groups and have several Sight Word Balls going at once. For a twist, allow children to stand (or sit on their desks) around the room and toss the ball to each other. Again, the word nearest a child's right thumb is the target word.

WHICH IS MY RIGHT THUMB?

For many children—not just struggling learners—mastering left and right is a challenge. I tried showing them how the thumb and index finger of the left hand make an L for "left." But for little guys who were still wrestling with reversals, that only muddied the waters. I tried putting a scrunchie on children's right wrist. Somehow, the scrunchie often ended up on the left wrist of fidgety young kids. I finally found a trick that worked.

I began to stamp everyone's right hand every morning. As part of our very structured morning routine, children would hand me their folder, and I would put the stamp of the week on their right hand (using non-toxic ink, of course!) and say, "Here is a _____ on your right hand."

Whenever possible, I used stamps to reinforce an instructional concept. When learning shapes early in the year, we had a week of my saying, "Here is a triangle (or square, circle, oval) on your right hand." Sometimes, the stamp would be a letter, and I would name the letter and sound as I stamped each student's right hand (or asked the stampee to name the letter and sound). That connection between "stamp" and "right hand" became so strong that eventually a stamp was no longer necessary!

We prepared for our Pledge of Allegiance every morning with these words: "My right hand goes over my heart." Children got so accustomed to looking for and raising their stamped hand that even after the stamp wore off (or was washed off by lunchtime), they would automatically glance at that hand when looking for "right."

The Sight Word Shuffle

Materials: set of sight word cards

Teach your children to play this game when they are with you in small groups and then allow the groups to play independently. Scatter the sight word cards facedown in a pile. Start moving the pile around while saying, "Pick a word, any word, pick a word NOW!" Each child pulls a sight word card from the moving pile.

Stop and ask each player to read the word on his or her card. If the student can read the word, he or she returns the card to the pile. If the student needs help reading the word, he or she keeps the card.

At the end of play, each child records the words from any cards he or she kept. The words can be recorded in a personal Word Journal. (See Pint-Sized Journals on the next page.) Since those are the words the child did not recognize, writing them provides additional practice.

PINT-SIZED JOURNALS

Children love little books, especially little books they can write in. But buying an endless supply of little notebooks for little hands is not in any of our budgets. Make your own never-ending supply out of simple, inexpensive materials. Better yet, ask older children in the building to make them for you or send the materials and instructions home for an eager parent volunteer—the parent who wants to help but can't come into your classroom on a regular basis. Most primary children won't be able to handle the task themselves.

You'll need the following:

- one or more sheets of paper: you can use the blank side of recycled paper
- one craft stick for each book
- one sturdy rubber band for each book
- a hole-puncher

Start with one piece of paper. As you use these little journals for more and varied purposes, you might want to use two pieces. Fold the paper in half and then in half again. Hold it like a book, with the long fold on the left. Use the hole puncher to put two holes, each about an inch and a half from the top (or bottom) and about a half inch from the left fold. Lay the craft stick across the holes. Once secured, it will serve as the binder of the journal. Thread one end of the rubber band from the bottom of one hole, through the hole. Slide the craft stick into the rubber band. Twist the rubber band once and pull it over the end of the craft stick, securing the stick. Repeat the process for the other hole.

You will have a journal with a front cover, two inside pages, and a back cover. For more pages, use scissors to cut the short fold. If you're using recycled paper, leave the fold intact so that the printed side of the recycled paper is not visible.

Again, you can also use two or more pieces of paper to make a thicker journal. Once you have a stack (or two) of these kid-friendly journals, you'll find lots of ways to use them. Younger children can use them for letter or number journals, filling each page with drawings or pictures cut from magazines. Older children can use them in guided reading groups to record new vocabulary, or they can use one per month for spelling words that give them trouble. All children can use them to record sight words they need to practice.

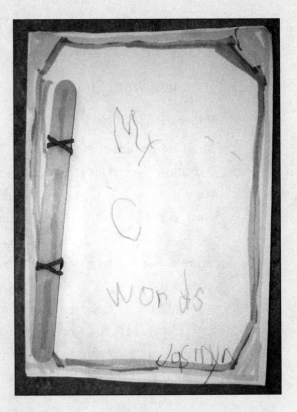

Pint-Sized Journals *Little folks love little books! These handy, inexpensive mini-journals will motivate and engage your budding authors.*

Early Reading Instruction & Intervention: A Sourcebook for PreK–2 © 2013 by Cindy Middendorf • Scholastic Teaching Resources

Stop the Mail

Materials: set of sight word cards, music selection to play

Use the laminated sight word cards that you've created for any of the other activities (e.g., Hopscotch, Musical Chairs). Ask children to sit in a circle on the floor, with every other child holding a sight word card. Each child reads the card to the players on either side of him or her. Play your music choice. When the music starts (or you say, "Send the mail!"), children pass the cards to the right. When the music stops (or you say, "Stop the mail!"), children hold their card for the rest of the circle to see and take turns reading the card to the group. Then the music begins, and mail delivery resumes. When children become comfortable with the procedure, try giving every child a card. As with the Sight Ball activity, you can divide your class into smaller groups.

Sight Word Bingo

Materials: computer-generated Bingo boards, dry-erase markers, erasers

Every early childhood teacher knows the power of bingo for practicing letters, numbers, classmate's names, color words, and sight words. Many years ago, I would spend hours and hours creating 25 bingo boards, making sure that no two were identical. And if I wanted the bingo boards in November to look different from those in March (more words, two-digit numbers, class initials or last names instead of first names), I had to spend more hours making a new set.

Much too late in my career, I learned how to make a class set of bingo boards in less than 10 minutes. I was probably one of the last teachers on the planet to discover how easy it is now to create functional bingo boards. (Too soon old, and too late smart!) For those who may still need the tip: Search the term "blank bingo board templates" on the Internet. You'll find a host of free Web sites that will allow you to design your own bingo boards. Many offer choices of 3-by-3, 4-by-4, or 5-by-5 grids, with or without a center "FREE" space. On most sites, you simply choose your template, type in the words or numbers you want in the boxes, enter the number of copies you want, and abracadabra! Bingo Boards, each set up differently.

If you print the bingo boards on standard copy paper, children can slide
tem into a plastic page protector (see page 57). With a dry-erase marker, they can
highlight each square to be covered and then erase the board to start again. No
more bingo chips dropping on the floor or becoming distracting noisemakers!

Sight Word Smorgasbord

In addition to the sight word interventions and supports described above, many of
the phonics activities outlined in Chapter 4 can also be powerful reinforcements
for sight-word instruction. The following engaging strategies can be effectively
adapted for sight word practice:

- Fun Phonics Placemats, page 73

- Tic-Tac-Go, page 76

- Four Sides, page 77

- KaBoom! page 79

- Towers, page 81

- Arm Spelling, page 83

- Configured Spelling, page 84

- Letter/Word Hopscotch, page 89

- Letter/Word Twister, page 90

- Musical Letter/Word Chairs, page 91

- Fly Away, page 91

- Letter/Word Blizzard Balls, page 93

CHAPTER 6

Vocabulary, Fluency, and Comprehension

I't's true, it's expected, it's natural. Literacy instruction in the early grades focuses on phonological awareness, phonics, and sight words. We practice; we drill; we decode and blend, decode and blend. Without mastery of those rudimentary skills, a child will not become a reader. However, reading a list of sight words or decoding and blending a stack of consonant-vowel-consonant words *is not reading*. The ultimate goal of all that basic instruction is to create readers of meaning—readers who can simultaneously decode, blend, process irregularities, infer tone of voice, visualize, and extract meaning from text that they can relate to themselves, to other texts, or to the world around them. Plain and simply: this is comprehension. And comprehension is dependent upon vocabulary and fluency.

"It is very important that the teacher have a definite objective in mind before attempting to teach reading. Reading is a necessary tool for use in the acquisition of all knowledge; something that a child must learn in the beginning of his school work, in order that he may use it in studying other branches."

—from *Practical Methods, Aids and Devices for Teachers* by Walter J. Beecher & Grace B. Faxon, Volume 1, 1916

What Do Tier 1 Teachers Need to Know About Vocabulary, Fluency, and Comprehension?

In recent years, a lot of research has focused on the ultimate goal of reading: extracting meaning and information that engages the reader. We know that the earliest decoders in kindergarten—those children who can efficiently sound out and blend together the phonemes in a word—are not necessarily the children who score the highest on third- and fourth-grade literacy assessments. Comprehension is sacrificed when children simply "bark at print." And while we must practice, reinforce, and teach and reteach phonics skills, we must also help children make the critical connection between text and meaning.

Quality Instruction and Interventions for Vocabulary

All children benefit from incidental and explicit vocabulary instruction, but our at-risk students must have focused, systematic instruction to give them the leg up they need for literacy success. Consider this sobering conclusion from a longitudinal study of vocabulary development in children:

> *By age 3, children from privileged families have heard 30 million more words than children from underprivileged families. Longitudinal data on 42 families examined what accounted for enormous differences in rates of vocabulary growth. Children turned out to be like their parents in vocabulary resources and language and interaction styles. Follow-up data indicated that 3-year-old measures of accomplishment in language predicted third grade school achievement.* (Hart & Risley, 2003)

Vocabulary development at age 3 predicted achievement in Grade 3! Vocabulary building is important for all children, but it is crucial for at-risk learners. Without intervention, lack of vocabulary will stunt literacy growth. We must imbed countless opportunities for vocabulary growth in our day, both as instruction and as intervention. Here are some ideas for doing that.

❖ **Change-a-Word:** For a dynamite shared writing activity, choose a simple sentence from a read-aloud or other text. Encourage children to replace words without changing the essential meaning of the text.
   Materials: read-aloud or another text, chart paper and marker

Change-a-Word *Challenge children to find powerful synonyms for words in a sentence.*

Early Reading Instruction & Intervention: A Sourcebook for PreK–2 © 2013 by Cindy Middendorf • Scholastic Teaching Resources

❖ **Ratchet Up the Teacher Talk:** Young children can understand the meanings of words that they would not use in their own speaking vocabulary, especially when those words are used in a context that supports meaning. Receptive language usually outpaces expressive language in children by many months. A 6-year-old, hearing an adult say, "That lunch was scrumptious!" quickly understands the meaning when he or she notices the adult smile and pat his belly. When we dumb down our conversational vocabulary with children, we neglect valuable teaching opportunities. Teachers, challenge your children (and yourself) by using words a tad more sophisticated than what children would use in their own dialogue. "You created this for me? The colors are stunning!" exposes the child to much richer vocabulary than "You made this for me? How colorful!" Be very conscious of the vocabulary you use in informal conversation.

❖ **Target Word Bank** Practice this strategy as a whole group before dividing the class into smaller, heterogeneous groups of four or five children. Choose a word from a book you've read or a theme you're studying. Begin with simple nouns. Write a target word on chart paper and invite children to brainstorm words that come to mind when they think of the target word. Use this for a shared writing lesson or for instruction on graphic organizers. Encourage children to brainstorm the most creative, unique words they can think of. A list may look like this:

house					
home	apartment	rooms	kitchen	pretty	address
sidewalk	roof	live	carpet	old	haunted
fancy	family	porch	comfy	bedroom	mansion

Then help children categorize the words according to nouns, verbs, or adjectives. Similarly, encourage them to group words that could be used to mean the same thing (*house, mansion, castle, trailer*).

Target Word Bank can also be played as an active game. Children can sit on desks or in a circle. Say a target word and then toss a sponge ball or other soft object to a child. That child names a word associated with the target word and tosses the ball to another child who names another association. At any time, allow a child to say "Pass."

Depending on the grade level and achievement level of your children, you can turn the Target Word Bank activity into a lesson on synonyms. As an editing activity for their writing, ask a child to create a Target Word Bank for one or more words and to replace a "penny word" (a word that is bland or overused) with a "fifty-cent word" (a word with pizzazz) from the word bank. Allowing children to choose a target word from their own writing builds self-assessment skills, too.

Materials: chart paper, marker, sponge ball or another soft object

❖ **Word of the Week:** An effective way to build vocabulary and reinforce classroom instruction is to highlight one word each week to be your "Wizard Word" or your "Standout Word" or whatever phrase you use to denote very special, noteworthy words. Because our youngest learners are so fascinated with language, learning a new word that is well beyond their speaking vocabularies gives them a welcome challenge and an opportunity to feel grown-up. Tie the words for a month to a theme (leading up to Earth Day, use *environment, citizen, endangered, pristine*). Or tie the words to character building (*compassion, self-management, empathy, restraint*). Post the word in your classroom. Take time each day to read the word, using it in sentences and spelling it. Encourage children to listen for and look for the word in conversations and print. And, of course, let parents know what the word of the week is!

❖ **Tri-Fold Words:** Give each child a strip of paper 4 inches wide and 18 inches long. Show them how to fold the strip into thirds, creating a tri-fold book. On the outside front cover of the tri-fold, each child writes a new, unusual, or assigned word. On the front inside flap, the child writes another word that means something similar to, or is associated with, the cover word. The middle section will have a sketch or drawing or picture cut from a magazine that helps define the cover word. In the last section, the child writes a sentence that uses that word. Leave the tri-fold books in baskets where children can access them. Challenge students to learn one another's words. Have a Friday afternoon "Vocabulary Showdown" where children read their synonyms and definitions and classmates guess the cover word. After a few weeks, let children create new tri-fold vocabulary strips.

Materials: 4-inch-by-18-inch paper strips, pencil, crayons, magazines, baskets

❖ **Tri-Fold Cut-Aparts:** Use the tri-folds from the previous activity. Let children cut apart their tri-folds. Put the panels from several children into a zippered plastic bag. At a center, children choose a bag and reassemble the tri-folds. Add a recording sheet that asks children to list each word they assemble and to write a sentence using that word.
Materials: Tri-Fold Words (from previous activity), scissors, zippered plastic bags, recording sheet

❖ **My Personal Dictionary:** Use the assembly instructions for Pint-Sized Journals (page 102) and have each child create his or her own dictionary. Students can decide which words to include in their monthly (or weekly) Personal Dictionary. Have them write the word, its meaning or a picture, along with a synonym in their Personal Dictionary. Encourage children to use the words in their dictionaries in writing and in speaking. Or children can create a thesaurus by writing one overused word on each page and listing richer, more colorful synonyms for it. As they write, they will become more and more aware of bland words and consult their personal dictionaries for more descriptive choices. Allowing children to use colorful fine-tip markers to create their dictionary pages guarantees engagement and reinforce retention.
Materials: Pint-Sized Journals, fine-point markers

❖ **Jazzing Up the Alphabet:** Use your Word Wall for more than just sight words. Get double the impact by also displaying, under each letter, three or four unusual or powerful words that you and children discover during read-alouds or content study. Write all the high-frequency sight words on cardstock of one color and put several blank cards of another color under each letter. Over the course of the year, challenge children to find enough "fifty-cent words" or "wow words" or "noteworthy words" to fill each blank card under each letter of the alphabet. Some may be words from content areas (*oviparous, incisor, tentacle*); others may be synonyms for overused words (*terrifying, stumbled, quipped*). Either way, your students will be focusing on words.
Materials: cardstock in different colors, marker

❖ **Word Venns:** Compare two or three new vocabulary words using a Venn diagram. Talk with children about number of letters, number of syllables, number of vowels, meaning, and frequency of these words in a given passage to compare and contrast. First and second graders can compare parts of speech, prefixes, and suffixes, too.

❖ **Nursery Rhyme Vocabulary:** Mother Goose rhymes are fanciful and imagery-filled. For readers with weak vocabularies, nursery rhymes offer an opportunity for enriching word knowledge in a fun-filled way, a way that immediately associates new words with nursery rhyme images. Think of the powerful vocabulary of those traditional, time-honored rhymes: "to *fetch* a pail of water," "broke his *crown*," "came *tumbling* after," "could eat no *lean*," "*rapping* at the windows," "one for the *dame*," "the sheep's in the *meadow*," "who *tends* the sheep," "gave them some *broth*," "sat on a *tuffet*," "*frightened* Miss Muffet away," "Mary, Mary, quite *contrary*," "Jack be *nimble*," "There was a *crooked* man," and so on.
Materials: Mother Goose and other nursery rhymes

Quality Instruction and Interventions for Fluency

Students who stumble over words, reread words several times, pay little or no attention to punctuation and phrasing, or read laboriously and with little expression are at-risk for being life-long poor readers (National Reading Panel, 2000). Fluency is the link between reading the words and making meaning and starts when children hear plenty of read-alouds delivered with generous voice inflection and conversational phrasing.

Fluency is best nurtured through lots and lots of supported oral reading. Round-robin reading, the favored strategy of decades ago, does *not* build fluency or comprehension. Quite the opposite! Research on round-robin reading suggests that it causes children to become stressed because they focus only on what they presume will be their assigned piece. Many of us have vivid memories of waiting with hearts pounding, scarcely hearing a classmate read while we nervously anticipated (and

> ## WHAT IS FLUENCY?
>
> The National Reading Panel considers fluency "the ability to read a text quickly, accurately, and with proper expression." Other experts expand the definition: "Fluency is the ability to read a text accurately and quickly. When fluent readers read silently, they recognize words automatically. They group words quickly in ways that help them gain meaning from what they read. Fluent readers read aloud effortlessly and with expression. Their reading sounds natural, as if they are speaking" (Armbruster, Lehr, & Osborn, 2003).

covertly rehearsed) the passage that we thought would be our part.

Actual fluency instruction, of course, cannot happen until children have a solid phonics foundation. Word recognition and decoding must be fairly automatic so that their mental focus can be on phrasing, noticing punctuation, and inferring tone of voice, rather than on decoding. Yet, even in preK and kindergarten, we can—and must—be laying the foundation for fluency. Supported oral reading takes away the "deer-in-headlights" reaction and demands the active engagement of all children. Since they get better at reading by reading, it makes sense to use the strategies that keep all children reading!

❖ **Modeled Fluent Reading:** Children learn to speak by being surrounded by and immersed in oral language. Likewise, they learn fluent reading through countless opportunities to hear text read with appropriate intonation, pauses, and feeling. Probably the most powerful intervention for children struggling with fluency is modeled reading. A well-done read-aloud engages every listener and allows children with limited literacy backgrounds to hear the flow, the expression, and the joy of reading. Whether reading fiction or informational text, we must realize that our oral reading sets the bar for the readers in our classroom. Use a variety of effective modeling strategies:

- teacher read-alouds
- taped read-alouds
- buddy reading (upper-grade children read to younger ones)

❖ **Choral Reading:** This powerful intervention for struggling learners is also an effective tool for honing the fluency skills of all learners. You already know that choral reading happens naturally when you come to the second or third reading of a Big Book that children love, especially those with patterned or repetitive text. The text for choral reading must be easy to see and to follow. For choral reading to be powerful for struggling readers, make sure that you (or a helper) are tracking the print with a pointer (moving smoothly from word to word, staying consistent with the voices). Teach children that you expect all eyes to be following the words, even if some of the words are difficult to decode.

Choral reading allows accomplished readers to showcase their skills, while enabling more hesitant readers to read as softly as they wish, receive immediate feedback on unfamiliar words, and realize that they can, indeed, read. Nonreaders and choppy, stumbling readers benefit from choral reading because it surrounds them with fluent reading, reinforces smooth matching of the printed word to the spoken word, and enables them to pay more attention to meaning since they are using less energy sounding out words.

Materials: display copy of easy-to-follow text, pointer

❖ **Choral Song Reading:** One of the best interventions for fluency comes from teaching struggling learners how to chorally "read" a song. Use the lyrics from a familiar song that children know and like. Write the lyrics in large print on poster paper or a whiteboard. (If you'll use the lyrics year after year, make a poster and laminate it.) Be certain to write the lines of text so that children can see the natural phrasing.

Teach children to read, instead of sing, the lyrics. Encourage lots of natural expression. Since children will most likely commit the words of the song to memory, even struggling readers will not have to expend brain energy on decoding. Instead, they can focus on fluent reading with appropriate phrasing and voice inflection.

Materials: display copy of familiar song lyrics

> ## FOR FLUENCY PRACTICE: TEXT MATTERS!
>
> Pay attention to the text you choose for fluency support and intervention. Use appropriate instructional-level text that most children will be able to read without frustration. When practicing fluency with the whole group, use memorized texts like nursery rhymes, songs, or previously read Big Books to allow all children to focus on prosody (rhythm, voice inflection, phrasing). Guided reading groups, with leveled readers, are a great venue for practicing fluency since a child's reading level is already matched with the text!

❖ **Echo Reading:** Echo reading, like choral reading, is a risk-free way to engage readers of all abilities. And as with choral reading, children must visually track each phrase, sentence, or line as it is read by the leader, and again as it is being echoed. Echo reading works especially well with poetry or nursery rhymes. You (or a competent, fluent student) read a line. The class tracks and reads the same phrase, line, or sentence using the voice pacing and inflection that you have modeled. In this way, children are hearing and immediately repeating fluent phrasing.

Materials; display copy of poem or nursery rhyme, pointer

Early Reading Instruction & Intervention: A Sourcebook for PreK–2 © 2013 by Cindy Middendorf • Scholastic Teaching Resources

❖ **Paired (or Assisted) Reading:** Paired reading is an excellent support strategy for all students, but it is an especially strong intervention for a child whose reading is choppy and disconnected. Expect exciting growth, especially when a struggling student is paired with a fluent reader, and the two have a respectful and supportive relationship. The pair works together to read together chorally or practice echo reading, or they can take turns reading sections.

When using paired reading as a one-on-one intervention, it helps to sit shoulder-to-shoulder with the child. Begin by reading chorally as a duet. Stop and allow the child to continue as long as he or she is maintaining fluency. Join in again as necessary.

Materials: suitable text for paired reading

> ### 5-MINUTE TAPES
>
> Blank cassette tapes with only 5 minutes of recording time on each side are available from most audio supply Web sites, and from several school supply sites. Just do an Internet search for "blank cassette tape 5 minutes." The tapes usually come in multi-packs and are relatively inexpensive.

❖ **Taped Reading:** If your concern is fluency, carefully consider the text when choosing books that come with CDs or tapes. While many are excellent for listening comprehension and building visualization (see page 119), some books can be too long and have too many words per page for young struggling learners who easily lose their place. It's often difficult to find leveled readers or books with simple text on tape or CD, but it's easy to create your own that you can use year after year.

Most schools still have tape recorders in the classrooms or tucked away in a dusty closet. For short readings, buy tapes that only hold 5 minutes worth of recording on each side. Ask a parent volunteer, the principal, a custodian, the music teacher, a cafeteria worker, or anyone whose voice children might recognize to record the book for you. Put matching stickers on the book and corresponding tape so students can locate them quickly or staple a plastic sandwich bag inside the back cover of the book and place the tape there.

For those of you fortunate enough to be in a school environment with lots of technology support, count your blessings! Today we can record books on CDs and a myriad of portable personal voice-recording devices. How the text is recorded and the equipment used to do so is not the important consideration. What's critical is a fluent reading of a simple, easy-to-track text that a child can follow!

Materials: text suitable for student reader, tape recorder, blank audio tapes, marker

❖ **Readers Theater:** Readers Theater is the dramatic reading of a script in which each reader reads a specific part. Emphasis is on the dramatic delivery of the text in speech patterns that accurately reflect the character. Parts are read, not memorized or acted. Readers Theater is a favorite activity for building fluency and for engaging even reluctant readers. You do not need props, costumes, or lighting, only a script.

Because children practice reading their lines from the script and also read from the script during the performance, the focus is on fluency and comprehension, and all students can be confident and successful. The central purpose is to help children develop reading that sounds natural and conveys meaning through voice inflection and intonation (and possibly gestures). You'll find that many of your students who need intervention for comprehension will love Readers Theater since the text comes alive, and they can read their lines just the way they hear the character in their head.

No time to turn favorite read-alouds into scripts for Readers Theater? No problem! Let some of your first or second graders work together to create a script. Or you can find dozens of free, ready-made scripts for all reading levels online (do a search for Readers Theater scripts) available for free download. You can also find scripts in numerous teacher resource books like *Readers Theater for Building Fluency* by Jo Worthy (Scholastic, 2008).

Materials: Readers Theater scripts

❖ **Family Fluency Practice:** The family is the first, best, and most powerful teacher for young children. As early childhood teachers, we recognize that. We work tirelessly to involve families in the early learning and to help children make connections between home and school. Realistically, we realize that not all children will have the advantage of a family who can or will spend the time and effort, but we continue to believe that with the

Early Reading Instruction & Intervention: A Sourcebook for PreK–2 © 2013 by Cindy Middendorf • Scholastic Teaching Resources

proper support, any family can be recruited to help us reinforce learning at home. Use the Parent Letter for Fluency to help parents understand the importance of supported oral reading at home and how to use effective strategies for doing so.

Certainly you will conference with, and send the letter to, the parents of any child who needs intervention for developing reading fluency. But consider sending the letter to *all* families, for supported oral reading at home not only builds fluency but also improves comprehension. Perhaps the most obvious advantage of a child's reading with a family member at home is simply the time spent together!

Materials: Parent Letter for Fluency (page 136)

❖ **Hearing Myself Read:** Use the 5-minute tapes described on page 113 to allow readers to hear their own reading and to assess their own fluency. It's not necessary to have them record an entire book. Simply reading into the tape for 3–5 minutes will capture the essence of his or her fluency. Put a date on struggling readers' tapes and save them. Repeat the self-taping in several weeks, and let children hear how they have progressed. Talk about motivation! Children can also hear themselves read when using a Whisper Phone as described on page 55. Unlike the taped self-reading, children cannot go back and analyze their reading, but practice shows that the immediate auditory feedback helps readers use more expression. In addition, comprehension improves!

Materials: text suitable for student reader, tape recorder, blank audio tapes, marker, whisper phone (optional)

❖ **You Read, I Read:** Hearing a passage read aloud by a fluent reader before attempting to read it independently is a powerful intervention for many children. You (or another competent fluent reader) should sit side-by-side with the child. The child tracks the text visually as the fluent reader reads and tracks with a finger or a pointer. Then the child reads the passage back, with support as necessary.

Materials: passage for reading aloud, pointer

❖ **Sentence Pyramids:** Draw a large pyramid on a sheet of paper and make a copy for each student or have students draw a large pyramid themselves. Then ask them to write one word or two words at the top. On the next line, have children write the first word again and add one or two more words to begin building a sentence. They can finish the sentence on the third line or create a fourth and fifth line. Ask children to go back and smoothly read each line. Let them exchange and read classmates' pyramids. Be warned! Some of your strongly verbal-linguistic children will take this activity to the extreme!

Materials: *chart paper, marker*

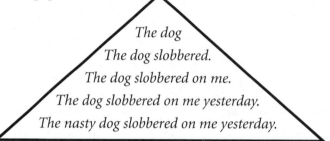

The dog
The dog slobbered.
The dog slobbered on me.
The dog slobbered on me yesterday.
The nasty dog slobbered on me yesterday.

Sentence Pyramid

Quality Instruction and Interventions for Comprehension

Comprehension is the elite, sophisticated goal of reading. In reality, comprehension is more a process than a skill. Of course, weaknesses in phonological awareness impede comprehension, and that requires interventions in phonemic awareness and phonics. But many children who can decode readily still have poor comprehension. Those who struggle with comprehension often have not mastered one or more of the following:

- listening comprehension

- visualization

- questioning

- thinking about meaning

Although all the comprehension activities and strategies described here provide quality instruction for all students, many children will need repeated and focused practice in using them. Guided reading groups provide a perfect venue for reinforcing comprehension strategies to the point where they become automatic.

Listening Comprehension: The Foundation for Reading Comprehension

We looked at the importance of teaching listening skills in Chapter 2. As we consider quality instruction for comprehension, we must again acknowledge the crucial role of listening because in the earliest grades, listening comprehension *is* the foundation for reading comprehension. And for very young readers who are hearing several read-alouds a day, listening comprehension *is* reading comprehension. If children can't attend to, respond to, focus on, and make meaning of text they hear in preK and kindergarten, then they will struggle with attending to, responding to, focusing on, and making meaning of text that they encounter in the grades that follow. We expect children to listen, but do we teach them *how* to listen? Train the "listening ears" of your students with some simple interventions.

❖ **Partner Repeats:** Take another look at this strategy that was outlined on page 43. When children know they are responsible for passing on a partners' thoughts, they quickly learn to listen to one another. Turn-Talk-Tell nurtures both receptive and expressive oral language skills.

❖ **What Does Listening Look Like?:** Too often we admonish our children, "You need to listen more carefully!" Some of our young students truly do not understand how to listen. Time spent modeling and practicing listening behaviors will pay big dividends. Use the I Am a Good Listener Poster to establish expectations and to teach your children what listening actually looks and feels like. Enlarge the poster, laminate it, and refer to it often. *Materials: I Am a Good Listener Poster, page 140*

❖ **Repeats and Paraphrases:** Your struggling students will benefit from paraphrasing what they have heard or been asked to do: "Michael, before you go to the Book Nook, tell me what I asked you to do there." When giving directions to the entire class, let students echo each step back to you. Ask children to turn to one or two talking partners and repeat the directions to each of them. Or, after giving the directions, ask them to "fill in the blanks" as modeled by Ms. K in "A Look Inside an Effective Tier 1 Classroom: Making Meaning Count," page 131.

❖ **Purposeful Listening:** Struggling learners, especially, need to know in advance that there is something in particular they must listen for. Before a read-aloud, give children several specifics to listen for; for example, ask them to listen carefully to hear how the mother felt when she learned of the problem or how many times the cow tried to get through the fence or who acted most responsibly at the park. Initially, ask children to listen for simple details but quickly advance to questions for which they must interpret text or draw inferences: "Listen and note why Peter was pretending not to hear." "Listen for the clues that will tell you why the little girl was gathering so many strange objects."

❖ **Listen and Draw:** Engage children often in a quick, 2- or 3-minute exercise that demands careful listening. Ask them to grab a piece of scrap paper and secure their listening post by putting a folder around their scrap paper or moving to a spot where their work will not be visible to others. Tell children that you will give each direction one time and one time only, and that they are to draw exactly what you dictate. As you give the directions, be sure to draw the graphic yourself so you'll have the accurate finished product to show. Make the directions specific, clear, and concise.

Once the drawings have been completed, hold yours so all can see it and let children declare themselves "an excellent listener!" or "an OK listener," or "a listener in need of improvement!" by drawing a happy face, a neutral face, or a sad face on their paper. Because this quick activity is for students to monitor their own listening skills, do not insist that they share their results. I have found that without exception, children improved each time we did this activity.

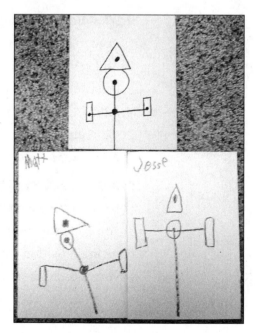

Listen and Draw *As children improve in listening comprehension, they are able to follow more detailed and specific oral directions. The picture at the top is the model.*

Early Reading Instruction & Intervention: A Sourcebook for PreK–2 © 2013 by Cindy Middendorf • Scholastic Teaching Resources

The photo on page 118 shows an example of a Listen and Draw scenario. The teacher drawing is on top, and two children's renditions are below. These are the directions the drawings were based on:

- "Put a dot somewhere near the middle of your paper."

- "Draw a triangle around the dot so that the dot is in the middle of the triangle."

- "Draw a circle under the triangle, touching the triangle."

- "Put a dot in the middle of the circle."

- "From the dot in the middle of the circle, draw a straight line to the bottom of your paper."

- "Put a big dot on that line, halfway between the top of that line and the bottom of that line."

- "Use that dot as the center of a line that goes from left to right, about 2 inches on either side."

- "Put a rectangle with the short side on top at each end of the left-to-right line."

This particular drawing involves more detailed directions than you would give to very young children or to children who were unaccustomed to this fast-paced listening activity. The children who produced the drawings in the photo were in May of their kindergarten year and had practiced Listen and Draw at least once a week for most of the school year.

Materials: scrap paper, crayons

Visualization: Comprehension Through Imagery

Visualization is the ability to form a mental image from words one has heard or text one has read. When I describe to you a shaggy, black dog wearing a wide, red collar that greeted me by putting his paws on my chest, you conjure up a mental image. One reader might picture a black Lab while another might picture a black mutt, but both put meaning to the text based on their own personal experiences, and both meanings are true to the text. Without the translation of words into mental images, reading is simply a process of naming words.

A consequence of our digital, highly technical, screen-filled world is that young children have less practice forming mental images than children of a generation ago. Today's infants and toddlers are bombarded with visual images, many of which are too fleeting for their brains to actually process. Yet, we know that children must learn to form personal mental images if they are to become readers of meaning. The National Reading Panel promotes imagery as an important piece of comprehension (NRP, 2000). Unlike the picture books that students encounter in the primary grades, the text in the upper grades will not always have illustrations that can be used to support comprehension.

All children need to learn that reading is more than naming words. Emphasize clearly and often that when we are reading, we must be thinking. Liken the process to having a clean whiteboard in our head. As we read, we write ideas or draw pictures that we get from the text. A good reader consistently practices making "brain pictures."

What can we early childhood teachers do to support this important ability to visualize and to intervene for children who have had little experience in imagining? As the activities below show, plenty!

❖ **Pictureless Reads:** Occasionally, read a story without showing the illustrations. Your strongly visual learners will be uncomfortable. They may beg to see the pictures or maneuver a way to peek at them. Explain that learning to make pictures in their heads is a step toward "grown-up reading." Let these children know that they can cover their eyes if it helps them see only what's in their brain and to listen better to the words.

❖ **Tapes and CDs Without the Books:** Listening centers are popular in early childhood classrooms; they provide valuable reinforcement as children follow printed text while listening to a recording of it. On occasion, remove the books from the listening center. Ask children to listen to the audio version and to make a movie in their minds based on the words they hear. Strongly visual learners may have trouble concentrating without a visual focus, just as they struggle with pictureless reads. Again, suggest they cover their eyes or provide scrap paper and crayons so they can doodle while they listen. You might ask them to draw what they are hearing. For many children (and adults!), having a visual focus, like doodling, makes it easier to listen. *Materials: audio version of a favorite text; crayons and paper (optional)*

❖ **Rich, Old-Fashioned Storytelling:** In the less frenzied years of the past, the tradition of oral storytelling was part of most children's early years. Families would gather around dinner tables and, without the background hum of television, would converse over a meal. Children would listen to parents and sometimes grandparents tell about the day's activities and adventures, visualizing the snake Grandma saw in the garden, the huge tire that came off a truck on the highway, the pile of paperwork on a desk, the grouchy clerk at the market. Students in your classroom who most need to hear folk tales, fables, and narratives of your experiences are those with the weakest oral language skills. But for all children, listening and telling stories is a powerful way to put muscle into visualization. Learn the old classics like Rapunzel and Rumpelstiltskin. Storytelling can calm the beast on a rainy day!

> ### THE RESEARCH ON STORYTELLING
>
> Brain research in the 21st century confirms that listening to stories, whether classic tales or stories of daily life, engages many parts of the brain, helps us form images based on language, and connects us to the experiences of others (Green, Strange, & Brock, 2000). A story well-told, even without props or visuals, empowers children to visualize as they interpret voice inflection, hear strong vocabulary, and watch a scene unfold in their mind.

Questioning: The What, Why, and How of Text

Students who regularly formulate their own questions about text, and then answer those questions, show improvement in comprehension (Oczkus, 2003). While it is important (and effective) for us to direct children to look for specific facts or inferences in the text before reading, it is equally crucial to ask readers to pose their own questions prior to reading. The widely used K-W-L charts are an effective tool to use to introduce readers to the process of wondering and asking questions about the text. As an intervention, teach children to make their own personal K-W-L chart based on looking at the book's cover, quickly flipping through the pages, or reading the inside book jacket or back cover blurb. Here are some specific ways to utilize a K-W-L chart.

❖ **Teach Questioning by Modeling:** Younger readers and readers with poor comprehension skills need frequent and deliberate modeling for questioning. When first teaching questioning skills, think out loud before you begin reading or assign a reading:

> *"The cover shows a snake. I wonder what kind of snake it is. I wonder what this particular habitat is on the cover. When I flipped through, I saw pictures of lizards and turtles. I'm pretty sure they're all reptiles. I wonder what all reptiles have in common. I wonder if all lizards live in the desert."*

Write key words or phrases from your questions on a whiteboard. As you read, put a sticky note on each page where a question is answered. Revisit the questions after reading, and use the sticky notes to find the answers in the text. It's important for children to understand that not all their prereading questions may be answered in the text.
Materials: whiteboard, sticky notes, pencils

❖ **News Photo Questions:** If children struggle with generating questions, begin by cutting out newspaper photos and accompanying captions. Fold the caption under so children see only the picture. Ask them to generate questions that they hope will be answered by the caption and then read the caption. Some questions will not be answered in the caption. Older readers could then read the article to find those answers.
Materials: newspaper photos and captions, scissors

❖ **My Photo Questions:** Ask children to bring in a snapshot from home that shows people or animals engaged actively. (Still shots of posed, smiling people won't elicit rich questioning!) Ask children to write (or dictate to you) a two- or three-sentence caption for the picture. Use these pictures in a lesson or during wait time to encourage children to ask questions about each photo and to determine which questions can be answered in the short caption. Once children learn to ask relevant questions about photos, remind them to use that same strategy when they approach a book or a passage.
Materials: snapshots featuring people and animals in action

Comprehension Strategies for Instruction and Intervention

Education in the 21st century demands that we encourage children, beginning in the early grades, to be critical thinkers, to go beyond multiple choice or recall answers, and to discern deeper meaning from text. We who teach the youngest grades know very well that children are capable of robust thinking but also that they must be coached to dig deeply. The following activities and strategies will help you get children to think about their own thinking, to extend story lines, and to bring their own experiences into a story.

Matt's Humpty Dumpty
Humpty Dumpty reclined on a brick fence.
Humpty Dumpty had an enormous accident.
The whole army—even all the knights and horses—
Could not fix him. Again.

Kamilia's Humpty Dumpty *Children practice retelling and vocabulary development using favorite nursery rhymes.*

❖ **Nursery Rhymes for Comprehension:**
We've looked at using nursery rhymes for developing vocabulary (page 110). Nursery rhymes can also be used to build comprehension and to help children understand what it means to retell a story in one's own words. Depending upon the level of your children, the retelling can be done orally or as an independent writing activity. Tell children they must include all the details from the original rhyme and stay true to the original meaning. Encourage them to simply rephrase each line, using as many "fifty-cent words" as possible. Practice as a whole class before turning the children loose. Mother Goose would be amazed at the creative versions of her old favorites! (This is a great introductory activity for Retelling With Round-Robin Story Talk, page 124). Note Matt's and Kamilia's adaptations of Humpty Dumpty at the left.

❖ **Thinking About My Thinking:** Even the earliest reading instruction has to include metacognition. Simply put, metacognition means that when I read, I think about what I am reading (or hearing), and my own understanding of it. I am constantly asking, "Does this make sense?" "What am I learning?" "What is the author trying to say?" "Do I understand this?" "What fix-up strategy do I need to use here?"

Readers who consciously focus their attention on their own thinking, fix their reading as they go and use a broad range of practiced strategies (like the ones we teach in guided reading) to become better readers of meaning (Israel, Block, Bauserman, & Kinnucan-Welsch, 2005). Use the I Know Good Reading Habits poster, page 141, to help your young readers develop metacognitive strategies.

❖ **Retelling With Round-Robin Story Talk:** Talking about text, especially through retelling, is a very powerful comprehension builder. When I have used the Story Talk strategy in my classroom, comprehension improved and children began making more comparisons among texts of similar genre or themes. An unexpected benefit was that they started paying closer attention to read-alouds and to guided reading texts, knowing that a Story Talk might follow. To my delight, children would even ask, "Can we story talk this book?"

Story Talk happens in a small group of four to six children, but only after you have modeled the strategy several times for the whole group, so that children have become expert facilitators for each other in reinforcing manners, taking turns, clarifying points, and offering interpretations. Children sit in a circle, and the child designated as the "Story Starter" begins by holding up the book so everyone can see it, then reading the title, naming the author, if possible, and giving just the briefest of description of the cover illustration. That child hands the book to the person on his or her right, and this first "Story Talker" turns to the first page of text, again holding the book for everyone to see. (Instruct children to bypass the title page, any acknowledgement pages, and so on.) In his or her own words, the child describes what is happening on these pages and what we learn from the pictures and/or the text. The book is passed to the right, and the next "Story Talker" turns the page and continues the story as shown on these pages.

Story Talk in Action: First Grade

Rylynn: I'm the Story Starter, so let's look at the cover. The title is *Make Way for Ducklings,* and a duckling is a baby duck, and "make way" means get out of the way and make room for them to come through. Duckling has *-ing* on it, like in the "king of ing." *(She points to the -ing in the word and hands the book to Stevie.)*

Stevie: *(turns to the first page of the story)* The mother and father duck have to move, but they can't find a good place to live 'cause the mother doesn't like any of the places the father likes, so they go to a city and find a pond. *(He hands the book to Jason.)*

Jason: You forgot to say the city is Boston. *(turns the page)* Anyways, the reason they liked this pond was 'cause it's in a park, and it had a big boat floating in it that had a big swan on the back of it, and the ducks thought the swan was real, but it was just a decoration on the boat. The people that were riding the boat gave the ducks food, so the ducks decided they liked this place. *(He hands the book to Geri.)*

Geri: *(turns the page and holds the book for all to see)* But they don't really like it when they get out of the water, because just then a kid goes by really fast on a bike and knocks the father duck on his tail, so they find another place not far away that was by water and she had babies, and they get to be friends with this guy.

Stevie: *(interrupting)* Michael, the cop.

Geri: Michael, the cop. And he feeds them breadcrumbs.

Stevie: *(correcting Geri)* No, peanuts. And the babies aren't hatched yet.

Geri: I mean peanuts. *(hands the book to her right)*

Angela: *(turns the page)* Um, and then, um, there's this river, and um, here's the bridge *(points it out in the picture)*, and, um, here's all the baby ducks that are hatched. Eight of them: *(points and counts)* 1, 2, 3, 4, 5, 6, 7, 8. They're all there, and so's the mama, but not the daddy, but I'm not sure where he is.

Several Students: He's out exploring. He went on a different trip. He's up the river.

(Angela hands the book to Rylynn, who was the original Story Starter.)

Rylynn: *(turns the page and continuing)* On Angela's page, she forgot to say all the rhyming names of the baby ducks like . . . *(turns back to the previous page, finds the words in the text, and reads)* "Jack and Kack and Lack and Mack and Nack and Ouack and Pack and Quack." Then, *(turns back to her page)* here's the page with the old-fashioned car and the policeman stopping it so the babies can cross the street. He heard them quacking so loud, and he wants other policemen to help, so—

Stevie: No, that's on my page next. *(takes the book from Rylynn and turns the page)*

If a group finishes its Story Talk, students should retell again, starting with a different person so that everyone gets to tell a different part. (The more you have practiced this strategy, the more effective it is.) To further enhance comprehension after Story Talk, have children make up a question to ask the others about the story. Or, as they finish, older children may pick up a sentence strip and begin writing the question they plan to ask. Remind students that their questions must begin with one of these words: *Who, What, Where, When,* or *Why?* Refer them to the Comprehension Wheel (below) for help in forming their questions.

❖ **The Comprehension Wheel:** We certainly do not have the time, nor do children have the interest, to dissect every read-aloud with detailed questioning, inferring, and summarizing, or to analyze plot, setting, character, problem, and main idea. Too much analysis can suck the joy out of reading! For quick comprehension mini-lessons, keep a Comprehension Wheel nearby. After a read-aloud, spin the wheel and focus on the element the arrow lands on. Consistent and frequent use of comprehension vocabulary (*plot, setting, characters, problem, sequence*) allows children to become comfortable and competent with the terms.

Materials: card stock, scissors, brad, marker

Comprehension Wheel *A quick spin and a quick discussion create a comprehension mini-lesson after a read-aloud.*

❖ **"Good Readers Look in the Book!":** As part of your post-reading comprehension activities when using Big Books, include one or more questions that require children to go back to the text to find the answer. Repeat this mantra, clearly and often: "Good readers look in the book!" The earlier we teach children to refer back to the text, the earlier they learn to skim text, think about beginning, middle, and end, and justify their answers.

For example, a read-aloud may begin, "The bluish sky was full of gray clouds that afternoon. Betsey raced past the old Donnelly place, vaguely aware of the scent from the lilacs." After the read-aloud, write a sentence (or paraphrase a sentence) from the text on chart paper or a whiteboard, leaving blanks for one or more words. (For the Big Books I use year after year, I prepare several sentences on poster paper, along with the words I intend to use, laminate them, and store them with the Big Book for easy retrieval.) Ask children to supply several words that would make sense in the blanks. Using the sentences in the above example, I could write the following sentences:

The bluish sky was full of _____ clouds that _____.
Betsey was _____ aware of the scent from the _____.

Together we would read following words, and briefly discuss any unfamiliar ones:

not	*lilacs*	*morning*	*Friday*	*roses*	*flowers*
vaguely	*soft*	*gray*	*afternoon*	*fluffy*	*hardly*

Children quickly realize that more than one word will make sense in each blank. But remind them to think about what the author said: "Good readers look in the book!" Ask children, "Should I go near the beginning, the middle, or the end of the book to find this part?"

This attention to text reinforces the importance of referring back to the author's words. When we ask children to engage in inference, a more abstract comprehension skill that requires readers to look for clues the

Word Bank and Text Sentences *The words (left) will be used to complete the sentences from the text (right). Since this activity will be used in following years, the words and text poster are laminated. The blanks on the poster have Velcro dots, as do the words in the word bank, making it easy to insert the word into the sentence.*

author has given, they will have had experience in going back to the text to find answers. Of course, the type of sentences and the number of blanks you leave will depend upon the level of your students.

Materials: Big Book, chart paper and marker or whiteboard

❖ **Main Idea:** Every early childhood teacher knows how difficult it is for children to boil down text to the main idea. Children with poor comprehension sometimes find and remember insignificant details of a story, but they can't connect those details to an overriding theme or idea. These children, in particular, need focused practice in finding the main idea. However, all children can improve their comprehension when they can clearly articulate the main idea or purpose of text.

Start small. Ask children to tell you the most important thing from a sentence or from a page that you've written or that you've taken from text. Use sentences with detail, like the following:

"After a while, time seemed to pass slowly for the pentagon and it became dissatisfied. 'I am tired of doing the same old things,' it grumbled. 'There must be more to life.' So the pentagon went back to the shapeshifter." (from *The Greedy Triangle* by Marilyn Burns)

"When people used to stop and watch them, Mike Mulligan and Mary Anne used to dig a little faster and a little better. The more people stopped, the faster and better they dug. Some days they would keep as many as thirty-seven trucks busy taking away the dirt they had dug." (from *Mike Mulligan and His Steam Shovel* by Virginia Lee Burton)

Choose a sentence, a selection, or a page, and have children decide what the author really wants readers to know. Use the terminology "main idea" as children learn to paraphrase and summarize ideas.

Use Aesop's fables to help children name the lesson or moral that the author wanted us to take away from the story. The moral of a fable *is* the main idea of the story, even if the words used to express it are not words from the story. As a bonus, the fables open discussion for character values and life lessons.

Whenever you read a picture book that has one underlying theme, encourage children to discuss the main idea: "What lesson does the author want us to learn? What was the author's purpose for writing this story? Can we say in a sentence or two what the main idea is?"

These class discussions of main idea can also become effective shared writing lessons. For example, students created a Class Book Report after reading *Morgan and Me* by Stephen Cosgrove. After partner talk, several children rephrased their partners' ideas of what the author wanted them to learn. Many said very similar things, in typical child-speak. Finally, I simply asked, "Many of you are saying very similar things. May I take all your words and rearrange them a bit?" They always agreed, and I then consolidated their thoughts into one or two sentences and asked if that summed up their idea of the author's lesson. Those sentences became an opportunity to share the pen. The names of two student illustrators were chosen randomly from a container. Although children had the option of declining the illustrator job, most eagerly grabbed the opportunity. The two illustrators then worked together to plan and draw an illustration that supported the summary.

Materials: Aesop's Fables or another text with a strong main idea, drawing paper, colored pencils or crayons

❖ **Book Talks:** A Book Talk is a literacy-rich oral-language activity that can be done at home or at school. Either way, children will be engaging with text, practicing retelling, and honing comprehension skills. At-risk learners get much-needed interaction with a book of their own choosing.

Book Talk at Home

Allow children to choose a book from your classroom or school library that you have read aloud to them. They take the book home and share it with a family member. The book should be short, easily read in one sitting, and have appropriate content and vocabulary for your grade level. Since the goal is to have children talk about the book instead of actually reading it, the reading level of their chosen book can be beyond their instructional level. Books may be fiction or nonfiction. If you are offering books from your classroom library, design a sign-out system to keep track of which child has which book. Let children practice retelling the events or content with one or more partners. Then send the books home with them for a Book Talk. Attach the Book Talk at Home parent letter on page 137 (or a similar certificate) to the book for parents to sign and return.

Book Talk at School

For this activity, children will again be retelling, sequencing, and summarizing. However, instead of preparing and practicing at school for a Book Talk at Home, they will prepare at home for a Book Talk at School. Well in advance, send home the Book Talk at School parent letter (page 138) with the date of child's Book Talk filled in.

Book Talk Writing Component

Depending upon the grade level and ability of your children, you may decide to include a writing component in the Book Talk. By asking children to complete the My Book Talk summary page (page 139), you can integrate writing into the activity. Younger children may need simpler versions of the My Book Talk report sheet.

By the time you begin Book Talks at school, you will have established a comfortable, supportive climate where peers listen respectfully to each other. In extreme cases, when a child is painfully shy or embarrassed by articulation problems, you might decide to ask him or her to do a Book Talk to one or two friends instead of the whole class, to you alone, to a puppet, or into a tape recorder.

Shannon's Book Talk *Kindergarten children use this simpler Book Talk Form.*

Early Reading Instruction & Intervention: A Sourcebook for PreK–2 © 2013 by Cindy Middendorf • Scholastic Teaching Resources

Making Meaning Count

As she sits in her rocking chair, Ms. K scans the class seated on the rug in front of her. She is using this Shared Reading time to introduce a unit from the science textbook and to offer literacy instruction and important literacy interventions for several children. As much as possible, Ms. K works to integrate content areas into all the literacy standards: reading, speaking, listening, and writing, as well as math standards.

Most children are seated shoulder-to-shoulder with their study buddy, one science textbook open between them. Ms. K knows that children will stay on track with text better when they are accountable to a partner.

Because his assigned study buddy is absent today, Nicky sits alone with his textbook. Ms. K makes a quick decision: Without a study buddy, Nicky will not get much out of today's lesson. She makes an intuitive assessment of who can best support Nicky in today's lesson.

Ms. K: Oh dear, Nicky, we're missing Kaila today. Your choice: Would you like to join Hettie and Sam, or would you prefer to be my study buddy today? (*Hettie and Sam look at Nicky expectantly. It's hard to tell whether they are excited or dismayed about the possibility of a third study buddy. But the children in this classroom have learned that everyone must respectfully support and cooperate with their peers, so if they're reluctant, they keep it to themselves.*)

Nicky: Can't I be by myself?

Ms. K: Make a choice, Nicky, unless you need me to choose for you: Hettie and Sam or me.

Nicky: (*with a resigned sigh*) I'll be their buddy. (*He moves to sit beside Sam as the other children adjust to make room for him. Nicky closes his own science textbook and puts it on the floor in front of him.*)

Ms. K makes no comment on Nicky's choice. Like all good teachers, she knows that sometimes less is more. Either choice was acceptable to her, and she knows Nicky well enough not to trigger a debate. Ms. K has worked diligently to establish safety and trust among classmates and her no-nonsense, assertive but gentle manner usually gets excellent results.

Ms. K begins the lesson with a very rhythmic call-together echo song (sung to the tune of "Are You Sleeping") that children know well. This transitions them to what Ms. K calls "our focus mode."

Ms. K: Are we ready?

Students: (*echo, using the same voice inflection*) Are we ready?

Ms. K: Yes, we are!

Students: Yes, we are!

Ms. K: *(pointing to her eyes, then her ears)* Eyes and ears are turned on.

Students: *(pointing to eyes, then ears)* Eyes and ears are turned on.

Ms. K: *(pretending to flip a switch on her head)* Brain's on, too. CLICK!

Students: *(pretending to flip a switch on their head)* Brain's on, too, CLICK!

Ms. K: Today the page turner and finger tracker will be the reader whose right shoulder is on the window side of the room. If you have three, the middle person is "It." *(She pauses for children to determine who will take that role.)* Page 47. When you and your study buddy have it, hook your own pinkies over your head, pull, and breathe deeply.

Students open their books to page 47. Two-by-two, arms go into the air. Each child locks his or her own pinkies together and gently pulls outward. Within a few seconds, all children are "pinky-locked," a strategy they know well. Ms. K knows that these few seconds of stretching will help Isaiah get the wiggles out and that all children will benefit from the rush of oxygen, as well as the activation of core muscles required to sit, stretch upward, and gently tug outward.

Setting the stage for the instructional activity to come (addressing Nicky, echoing the focus chant, finding the page, doing the finger-lock) took less than 2 minutes. Ms. K, a typical early childhood teacher, always feels there's never enough time. But she also knows that simple, comfortable routines calm children, raise the levels of positive neurotransmitters in their brains, and pay huge dividends for the time invested.

Ms. K: Get ready to read the title together. 1, 2, 3. *(Children point to the title words in their book.)*

Ms. K and Students: (in unison) What is beyond the sky?

Jamiha: Ooooh, it's about outer space.

Gregory: Yeah, like alien stuff.

Ms. K: *(except for giving Jamiha and Gregory "the eye," Ms. K ignores their comments.)* Share everything that you already know about outer space with your study buddy.

Children turn to their buddies to eagerly share ideas and experiences about movies they've seen and stories they've heard. Ms. K allows about 60 seconds for this, knowing that the time to access prior knowledge is important, even when children are talking about fictional accounts of a topic. From past experience, she understands that this unit will address a lot of children's misconceptions about outer space. Ms. K makes a call-back sound (a rhythmic hand clap that the children echo).

Ms. K: Now, my friendly space explorers, you and your study buddy need to look at and talk about the three pictures on pages 47 and 48.

Immediately, the room again fills with a busy hum as children pore over, comment on, and speculate about the photographs in the textbook. Ms. K's trained ear catches a phrase here, a question there, a buddy reading a caption or pointing out a picture detail.

Ms. K: *(after about a minute)* Ten seconds left! 9, 8, 7, 6, 5, 4, *(more and more children stop their discussions and join the countdown)* 3, 2, 1. Done! Point to the caption under the picture in the lower left on page 48. Sentence by sentence, echo me.

Echo reading is very familiar to the children. Ms. K reads the first sentence, and children echo the text as the finger pointer in each set of study buddies tracks the print. The same procedure is used for the second sentence of the caption. It is a longer sentence, so Ms. K stops midway for children to echo.

Ms. K: Finger in, book closed! *(Children know this procedure. The finger pointer holds his or her finger between the pages, but closes the book, holding the place.)*

Ms. K: Get caught on thought. *(This is another procedure that has been well practiced. Children close their lips tightly to make sure no words escape, and they really concentrate. Some close their eyes.)* When did the first American go into space? *(Ms. K pauses for 2 or 3 seconds, allowing everyone to think. Then she gives the cue for a choral answer.)* 1, 2, 3!

Nicky, Mel, Charesa, Sam, and Others: *(all at once)* 1961! 1969! 1961! 1900! A long time ago!

Ms. K: *(smiling, with eyebrows raised)* Good readers . . .

Students: *(in unison)* Look in the book!

Books open, study buddies skim the pictures and captions, and fingers point to the date. Children point it out to each other. Several smugly pat themselves on the back. Ms. K doesn't need to say a word. She turns her book where all can see that she has a small piece of colored highlighting tape over the date in one caption. Very quickly, all fingers point to the date in their own books.

Ms. K: Together read the date. (*Children respond, and Ms. K writes it in the corner of her whiteboard.*) We need to remember this. Later we'll calculate how many years ago that was, and if anyone we know might have been alive then. But for now, listen up!

At that practiced cue, all eyes turn to her. Children visibly straighten their backs, except for Debra. Ms. K gives a smile and a wink to Debra's study buddy, Mel, and a nod toward Debra. Mel gently touches Debra's arm and points to Ms. K. Debra sit up straight.)

Ms. K: You and your buddy will go to your reading spots. Read pages 47 and 48. You decide whether you will chorally read together, echo read, or partner read the pages. When you've finished the first read-through, choose another way to read the pages, and read them again. Finally, you and your buddy will each think of one question you have about outer space, one "I Wonder" question. Help each other write your "I Wonder" on one of the colored index cards from the green basket. Put your question cards in the I Wonder box.

Ms. K knows that at this point in the year, her children, with help from one another, can write their questions. Earlier in the year, she allowed children to speak their questions into a tape recorder. Either way, listening to one another's questions sparks conversation!

Ms. K: Let's make sure we all know what to do! You and your study buddy will go to . . .

Students: Our reading spot!

Ms. K: And you will read pages . . .

Students: 47 and 48.

Ms. K: And how will you read today?

Students: *(Answers vary, but all are correct.)* We choose! Choral or echo or partner! Any way we decide!

 Early Reading Instruction & Intervention: A Sourcebook for PreK–2 © 2013 by Cindy Middendorf • Scholastic Teaching Resources

Ms. K: After you read it once, you must . . .

Students: *(again, a variety of answers, all correct)* Read it again! Read it a new way! Pick another way to read it!

Ms. K: And then each of you must . . .

Students: Think of a question.

Ms. K: And write your questions . . .

Students: On colored cards.

Ms. K: You'll find the colored cards . . .

Students: In the green basket.

Often when Ms. K gives a series of directions, she carefully structures an opportunity for children to repeat the directions back to her. She usually moves toward Nicky and Corey, who both need intervention to build listening skills and the ability to follow multi-step directions.

Ms. K is confident that the 5 to 6 minutes just spent on prereading will give her children a solid foundation for the science reading they are about to do. For the next 10 to 15 minutes, study buddies read and reread, discuss and write questions. Because Ms. K has established consistent routines in the room, children know exactly what to do when they and their study buddy are finished. Soon, all children are busily engaged in more reading: Some are perusing the books from the baskets at their table, some are in the Book Nook using whisper phones to read stories or "read pictures" to themselves, some are partner reading favorites from the read-aloud basket. Most, however, are on the rug, looking at, ogling, and quietly discussing the dozen or so outer space books that Ms. K quietly spread there. This variety of material, from picture books to seriously detailed informational texts and magazines, will remain in the room during the study of the science unit on space.

Parent Letter for Fluency

Date: _____

Dear Family,

Research shows that all children grow in reading skills—by leaps and bounds—when they practice reading at home. In these early grades, when your child is learning to decipher words and put meaning to them, there are several ways that you can ensure your child's success.

I know how busy family days and evenings are. I also know that you are the best, the most powerful, the most impressive teacher your child will ever have. By spending 10 minutes a day doing any of the activities described below with you, your child will measurably improve his or her reading achievement.

Fluency is the ability to read smoothly, at a reasonable rate, and with expression. When a child reads haltingly, or spends most of the time figuring out words, meaning gets lost; he or she ends up not understanding any of the text. These research-based activities will improve fluency and therefore comprehension. Be sure to use a book that is relatively short and at a comfortable independent reading level for your child. (I can recommend and send home appropriate books.) Just ask!

1. **Read-alouds:** Your child needs to hear reading that is smooth and delivered with expression. Experts agree that regularly hearing books read with expression improves children's reading achievement dramatically.

2. **Echo reading:** Choose a book with only one or two lines per page. Read the text to your child while tracking the words with your finger. Then ask your child to echo by looking at the words, tracking each line with his or her finger, and reading it with the same phrasing and expression that you used.

3. **Choral reading:** Snuggle side by side, so both you and your child can easily see the pages. Follow the words with your finger, a pencil point, or a small pointer underneath and read them along with your child.

4. **Paired (or assisted) reading:** Read the pages together, with your child moving a finger under each word. At some point, stop and allow your child to continue reading, still following each word with his or her finger. If your child makes a mistake, move his or her finger back to the misread word and start reading along again. Stop and start as necessary.

5. **Repeated reading:** Practice makes permanent! The more your child reads a passage, tracking the text with eyes and an index finger, the smoother the reading. The smoother the reading, the better the understanding. Instead of asking your child to read a lengthy passage once, choose shorter passages and ask for several readings.

Simply 10 minutes a day will pay off in big reading rewards! Be sure to discuss and ask your child questions about the book as you read. Rereading the same story is great for building fluency and confidence. Most of all, enjoy these one-on-one moments with your blossoming reader!

Partners in Learning,

_____

Early Reading Instruction & Intervention: A Sourcebook for PreK–2 © 2013 by Cindy Middendorf • Scholastic Teaching Resources

Book Talk at Home

Date: _____

Dear Families,

Today your child is bringing home a book for a Book Talk at Home. Please sit with your child for about 5 minutes as he or she turns the pages and tells you the story or facts from the book. Talking about the book and "reading the pictures" is an important step in building reading skills that will help your child read books without picture clues in the future. Ask questions and discuss the story as you feel it is appropriate. Remember, the task is not to read the words but to tell the story. Of course, if you'd like to read the book to your child as tonight's bedtime story, that's a bonus! And, if your child is able to read it to you, even better!

Research confirms that children who can retell stories or summarize books are well on their way to a successful school experience. Thanks for helping to lay this important foundation for your child to become a successful reader!

Please send the book and the certificate on the bottom of this page back within three days.

Partners in Learning,

_____

Hooray!

_____ completed a Book Talk at Home.

The title of the book is _____

_____ .

Signed _____

Book Talk at School

Date: _____

Dear Families,

Reading experts constantly remind us that the more children handle, enjoy, talk about, and interact with books, the more likely they are to become successful, life-long readers and learners.

Next month, we'll be starting the first of our Book Talks at School. (You've already heard a Book Talk at Home.) This is the foundation for traditional book reports that your child will be asked to do in future grades. Your child will choose a book to "picture read" at home by telling the stories in the illustrations, (and perhaps hear it read aloud). On Book Talk Day, he or she will tell the class about the plot, characters, and setting. Please encourage your child to be prepared for Book Talk Day. Most likely the class will *not* have heard this story before, so we will be looking to your child for the summary! One child will report each day. Attached is the schedule for our first round of Book Talks. (We'll do other rounds later in the year.)

Your child can choose to talk about a book that is borrowed from our classroom, taken out of the local library, or chosen from the favorites at home. Please encourage your child to practice at home what he or she will tell the class about the book. The Book Talk should include information about the author and illustrator, who or what the book is about (the characters), where it takes place (the setting), and a short summary of what happens (the plot). A Book Talk typically lasts about 3 to 4 minutes. Encourage your youngster to decide the most important ideas in the book, and not to include every little detail.

Ask your child to complete the attached My Book Talk report sheet. The summary section should be a combination of words and illustration. Your child can do the writing or dictate the words for you to write. Thank you for your continued support in moving our children along on the Literacy Train!

Partners in Learning,

_____

Early Reading Instruction & Intervention: A Sourcebook for PreK–2 © 2013 by Cindy Middendorf • Scholastic Teaching Resources

My Book Talk Summary

My name is _____ .

The title of my book is _____ .

The author of my book is _____ .

The illustrator of my book is _____ .

About my book:

_____

_____

_____

_____

This is an illustration that tells about my book:

I Am a Good Listener

✔ I face the speaker.

✔ I sit up straight and still.

✔ I look at the speaker's eyes and mouth.

✔ My brain is on.

✔ My voice is off.

✔ I listen for important words.

Bats are mammals that fly. They fly at night.

Bats and mammals

I Know Good Reading Habits!

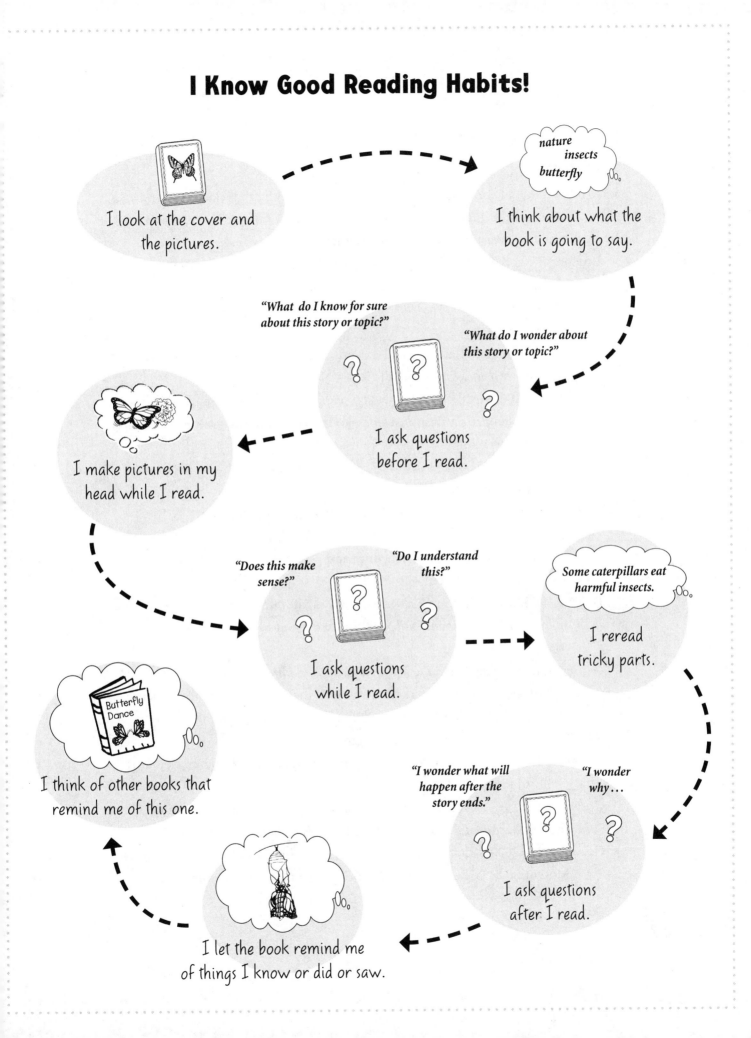

References

Armbruster, B., Lehr, F., & Osborn, J. (2003). The building blocks of reading and writing in *A child becomes a reader: Proven ideas from research for parents.* (2nd ed.).Washington, DC: The Partnership for Reading.

Beecher, W. J., & Faxon, G. B. (1916). *Practical methods, aids and devices for teachers* (Vol. 1). Dansville, NY: F. A. Owen.

Block, C., & Israel, S. (2004). *Reading first and beyond.* Thousand Oaks, CA: Corwin Press.

Carnine, D., Silbert, J., Kame'enui, E. J., and Tarver, S. G. (2004). *Direct instruction reading.* (4th ed.). Upper Saddle River, NJ: Pearson.

Catts, H. W. (2006 April). "School-wide screening." Presentation at the National SEA Conference on Responsiveness to Intervention: Integrating RTI Within in SLD Determination Process. Kansas City, MO.

Cotton, K. (1988). *Classroom questioning.* Portland, OR: Northwest Regional Education Laboratory.

Dennison, P. (2006). *Brain gym and me.* Ventura, CA: Edu-Kinesthetics, Inc.

Diamond, A. (2000). Close interrelation of motor development and cognitive development and of the cerebellum and prefrontal cortex. *Child Development, 71*(1), Jan.–Feb., 2000, 44–56.

Feder, K. P., & Majnemer, A. (2007). Handwriting development, competency, and intervention. *Developmental Medicine and Child Neurology.* April: 49(4) 312–317.

Getting ready: Findings from the National School Readiness Indicators Initiative: A 17 state partnership. (2005). Sponsored by the David and Lucille Packard Foundation, the Kauffman Foundation, and the Ford Foundation. Retrieved October 16, 2011 from www.gettingready.org.

Gillan, G. T. (2004). *Phonological awareness: From research to practice.* New York: Guilford Press.

Goswami, U. (1999). Causal connections in beginning reading: The importance of rhyme. *Journal of Research in Reading, 22*: 217–240.

Goswami, U. (2000). Phonological and lexical processes. In M. L. Kamil, P. B. Mosenthal, P. D. Pearson, & R. Barr (Eds.). *Handbook of reading research.* Vol. 3 (pp. 251–267). Mahwah, NJ: Erlbaum.

Green, M. C., Strange, J. J., & Brock, T. C. (Eds.). (2000). (2002). *Narrative impact: Social and cognitive foundations.* Mahwah, NJ: Erlbaum.

Hannaford, C. (2007). *Smart moves: Why learning is not all in your head.* (2nd revised ed.). Atlanta, GA: Great Ocean Publishers.

Hart, B., & Risley, T. R. (2003). The early catastrophe: The 30 million word gap by age. *American Educator, 27*(1), 4–9.

Hausner, M. E. (2000). The impact of kindergarten intervention project accelerated literacy on emerging literacy concepts and second grade reading comprehension. Paper presented at the Annual Meeting of the American Educational Research Association. Seattle, WA, April 10–14, 2001.

Hull, R. H. (2010). Why children may give you a blank look when you teach them something new: The emerging CNS auditory system in children. Presentation at the OSEP, U.S. Department of Education Project Directors Conference. Washington, DC.

International Reading Association. (1997). The role of phonics in reading instruction. A position paper of the International Reading Association. Newark, DE: IRA Board of Directors.

Israel, S., Block, C., Bauserman, K., Kinnucan-Welsch, K. (Eds.). (2005). *Metacognition in early literacy.* Mahwah, NJ: Erlbaum.

Jensen, E. (2005). *Teaching with the brain in mind.* Alexandria, VA: Association for Supervision and Curriculum Development.

Jensen, E. P. (2007). *Introduction to brain compatible learning* (2nd ed.). Thousand Oaks, CA: Corwin Press.

Koziatek, S. M., & Powell, N. (2002). Pencil grips, legibility, and speed of fourth-graders' writing in cursive. *American Journal of Occupational Therapy, 54,* 9–17.

Le Roux, T. (2009). *Fine motor activities to help your children: Correct pencil grip.* Retrieved May 5, 2011 from www.ot-mom-learning-activities.com.

Manset, G., St. John, E. P., Simmons, A. B., Worthington, K., Chung, C., & Manoil, K. (2000). *Indiana's early literacy intervention grant program impact study for 1999–2000.* Bloomington, IN: Indiana Education Policy Center at Indiana University.

Marzano, R., Pickering, D., & Pollock, J. (2001). *Classroom instruction that works: Research-based strategies for increasing student achievement.* Alexandria, VA: Association for Supervision and Curriculum Development.

Meaden, H., Stoner, J. B., Parette, H. P. (2008). *Sight word recognition among young children at-risk: Picture-supported vs. word-only.* Assistive Technologies Outcomes and Benefits, Vol. 5, 1.

National Reading Panel. (2000). Teaching children to read: An evidence-based assessment of the scientific research literature on reading and its implications for reading instruction. Washington, DC: National Institute of Child Health and Human Development.

Oczkus, L. D. (2003). The four reciprocal teaching strategies. In *Reciprocal teaching at work: Strategies for improving reading comprehension.* Newark, DE: International Reading Association.

Rowe, M. B. (1987). Wait time: Slowing down may be speeding up. *American Educator, 11,* 38–43, 47.

Schunk, D. H. (1986). Verbalization and children's self-regulated learning. *Contemporary Educational Psychology, 11,* 347–369.

Snow, C., Burns, M., & Griffin, P. (1998). *Preventing reading difficulties in young children.* Washington, DC: National Academy Press. Available online at http://books.nap.edu.catalog/6023.html.

Stahl, R. J. (1990). *Using think-time behaviors to promote students' information processing, learning, and on-task participation: An instructional module.* Tempe, AZ: Arizona State University.

Velluntino, F. R., Scanlon, D. M., & Tanzman, M. S. (1998). The case for early intervention in diagnosing specific reading disability. *Journal of School Psychology, 36,* 367–397.

White, T. G. (2005). Effects of systematic and strategic analogy-based phonics on grade 2 students' word reading and reading comprehension. *Reading Research Quarterly, 40*(2), 234–255.

Wilkins, A. (2003). *Reading through colour: How coloured filters can reduce reading difficulty, eye strain, and headaches.* West Sussex, England: John Wiley & Sons, Inc.

Worthy, J. (2008). *Readers Theater for building fluency.* New York: Scholastic.